BROKEN ROADS

BROKEN ROADS

RETURNING TO MY AMISH FATHER

IRA WAGLER

New York Nashville

FaithWords
Hachette Book Group
1290 Avenue of the Americas, New York, NY 10104
faithwords.com
twitter.com/faithwords

First Edition: May 2020

FaithWords is a division of Hachette Book Group, Inc. The FaithWords name and logo are trademarks of Hachette Book Group, Inc.

The publisher is not responsible for websites (or their content) that are not owned by the publisher.

The Hachette Speakers Bureau provides a wide range of authors for speaking events. To find out more, go to www.hachettespeakersbureau.com or call (866) 376-6591.

Library of Congress Cataloging-in-Publication Data
Names: Wagler, Ira, author.
Title: Broken roads : returning to my Amish father / Ira Wagler.
Description: New York, NY : FaithWords, 2020.
Identifiers: LCCN 2019049242 | ISBN 9781546012061 (trade
    paperback) | ISBN 9781546012054 (ebook)
Subjects: LCSH: Wagler, Ira. | Ex–church members—Amish—
    Biography. | Fathers—Death. | Wagler, David.
Classification: LCC BX8143.W22 A3 2020 | DDC 289.7092 [B]—dc23
LC record available at https://lccn.loc.gov/2019049242

ISBN: 978-1-5460-1206-1 (trade paperback), 978-1-5460-1205-4 (ebook)

Printed in the United States of America

LSC-C

10 9 8 7 6 5 4 3 2

This book is dedicated to my father,
David L. Wagler.
He was a giant among his people.

CONTENTS

Prologue   1

Present   5

Past   13

Daviess and Vincennes   19

Summer in Lancaster   34

Bob Jones University   44

Home for Christmas   60

Law School   69

Ellen   80

Wedding   88

CONTENTS

Stone Angel   94

March Is the Cruelest Month   103

The Long Good-Bye   111

Stone Angel Redux   116

Returning to My Father   126

Reuben and Me   139

Mom's Funeral   150

A Day That Will Never Come   177

Whiskey and Me   186

Back to the Present   202

The Past and Dad's History   213

Dad's Funeral and Final Thoughts   223

Acknowledgments   255

About the Author   257

BROKEN ROADS

To lose the earth you know, for greater knowing; to lose the life you have, for greater life; to leave the friends you loved, for greater loving; to find a land more kind than home, more large than earth —

—Whereon the pillars of this earth are founded, toward which the conscience of the world is tending—a wind is rising, and the rivers flow.

—*Thomas Wolfe*

PROLOGUE

THE AMISH HAVE been around for a long, long time. Hundreds of years. Today, around three hundred and thirty thousand of these incredibly unique people are scattered throughout the United States and Canada. Out of seven-plus billion people in the world. For such a small group, they have a tremendous presence in English society—not only in North America but globally. They are much romanticized, but that's not their fault.

I was born one of them. Ira Wagler, the ninth of eleven children of David and Ida Mae Wagler, who emerged from the remote and rather despised Amish community in Daviess County, Indiana. I was the fifth son of a fifth son. My parents fled Daviess, as Dad was convinced the place was going bad. He didn't want to raise his family there. So I grew up among my people in smaller communities. It was a long hard road, to break away. I guess I'm the one who remembers and who talks about things a lot, things that happened long ago. I wrote the

1

story of my journey in my first book, *Growing Up Amish,* published in 2011.

Until my father and a few of his peers launched Pathway Publishers in the 1960s, the Amish never had much of a voice of their own. With *Family Life* magazine and the other Pathway publications, that voice was presented in a coherent structure for the first time. It was an extraordinary achievement. Nothing like that had ever been attempted before. My father and his peers had a vision and pursued it. With unceasing labor, at great financial risk, and with potential loss of prestige. The venture succeeded beyond their wildest imaginations.

They published a lot of good, solid stuff, especially on historical subjects, and common-sense articles on farming and other issues of specific interest to the Amish. And yet I have always felt that the fictional writings and op-eds published by my father and others at Pathway were less than honest. Too much gooey mush. Too didactic. Too pat. Too formulaic and predictable. All the same answers, all the time. All the loose ends neatly tied up in a little package for the reader to remember.

Maybe they were projecting a moral ideal they knew was impossible. I think they were trying to live that ideal, too. To present themselves and their community as an example. But it's impossible to be perfect. You can't be a shining city on a hill by proclaiming your own greatness and glory. And real life isn't a nice little list of neatly packaged formulas, either. Never has been. Never will be.

Over the years, I have wondered many times if my father and his contemporaries ever questioned the path they chose. The God they served. Did they ever despair that He exists? Question their faith? Or was it always cut and dried, black and white? When their children left and they cut them off cold, did it not tear at them deep inside? The hard, ruthless laws of shunning, did they ever think twice about them? And wish it were not so? Did they ever struggle with such issues? Or did their harsh, cold facades truly reflect their hearts?

I like to think they struggled sometimes. Weren't so sure of themselves. It would have been human. But I don't know that. Because they never told us. Maybe they thought it would show weakness. It wouldn't have. To the contrary, it would have shown strength. And honesty.

And I think, too, of my grandfather, Joseph K. Wagler. My father's father, a man I never met. Because he died when my father was young. What kind of man was he? I'll never know. Nothing was ever told, other than the vacant, shallow depictions of a stern, godly father and deacon in the church. There is so much more I wonder about. How he looked. The man he was in the community. As he labored in the fields among his children. The sound of his voice when he prayed the morning prayer and read Scripture aloud in church. What gave him joy? And what were his quirks?

And my great-grandfather, Christian Wagler, who shot himself in the chest back in 1891 when he was thirty-six years old. His destitute widow remained, and his young sons and daughters. Christian was buried as a lost soul, there in the Stoll graveyard in Daviess County, Indiana. They knew, the Daviess people, that he was damned to burn in the fires of hell for all eternity. They knew, too, that the shameful stain of his suicide would haunt his seed forever.

Who was Christian? There are no photos. How did he look? Tall or short? And the demons he faced, in the dark recesses of his tortured soul, that finally overwhelmed him. Why did he do it? How was his last morning? What were his last words?

I'll never know. I can only conjecture, because no one ever honestly wrote the details at the time. And I accept that. It's who they were. Some things were just not done. Some layers not peeled back, the dark secrets carefully guarded. The old way, of the old generations.

But they left us poorer for our lack of knowledge of who they were. And who we are. Every culture and every generation brings forth its giants and its common people. Its common stories. Its tragedies. And its epics. But the characters involved cannot be seen and will not be heard and will be forgotten if no one speaks their names.

And tells of them. As they were. In their struggles. Their triumphs. With their flaws. Their impossible visions. Their failures. And their shining accomplishments. As they marched across the stage on which we now play our own roles.

That's why I write.

PRESENT

IT HOVERED OVER us like a dark and looming cloud as the holidays approached. December of 2018. The restless winds stirred, we knew that my father was old and very sick and wasting away. He had been around for a long, long time. Ninety-seven years. There wasn't a lot we hadn't seen, not when it came to his health. He had dipped down before, he had drifted to the edge of death's door more than once. But he had always pulled back somehow. He had always returned to attack life as only my father could. Until now. This time, it was different. This time, he kept sinking lower and receding faster as the days slipped by, and then the weeks. Until it became clear to all of us. Dad had reached the end of the road. This time would be the last time.

Time doesn't stop. It never has, and it didn't then. Before we knew it, Christmas was knocking on the door. And I wanted to celebrate with friends, to exult in the great joy of all that Christmas is and all it means. And I also knew my father was on his deathbed and would never rise again. It was a formula that yanked my emotions from one side far away to the other. Rolling and pitching around. I've learned over the years. In such a time, just keep walking. It's the only option that makes sense. If you don't know what else to do, keep walking. And so I did.

Christmas Day. I always sleep in. I got up late and puttered about. Got my free coffee at Sheetz, a popular chain convenience store not far from my house in Lancaster County, Pennsylvania. They give away their watery black brew on Christmas Day and New Year's Day. You can just walk in and help yourself and wave at the clerk. Soon after eleven, I was ready to head over to my older brother Stephen's house for lunch, a ten-minute drive to the other side of Leola. A big old Christmas meal, they always serve there. I parked and walked in, holding a bag with a box of assorted Gertrude Hawk chocolates for Wilma. That's my usual gift to my brother's wife. The family, the sons and daughters, had arrived earlier to exchange gifts. And right at noon, we all sat around the large table in the dining room and enjoyed lots of rich good food. We sat around and talked afterward. Of course, Dad came up in the conversation. That and my trip the next day.

"I'm packing tonight," I said. "Loading my Jeep. Tomorrow, early, I head out, up to Aylmer." That was where Dad was. Back in the land of my birth. Stephen and Wilma wished me safe travels and told me to keep the family informed. I promised I would.

At home, I took my time. Dragged out my big old suitcase and got started packing. Ellen and I bought a set of bright-red soft-shell roller luggage many years ago. She took the cute little carry-on suitcase with her and left me the big one. It was all pretty laid back, how we divided things like that. My big red suitcase has been beaten around a good bit, from airline abuse and general wear and tear. The zipper gets stuck sometimes. It's more than fifteen years old, which is probably old for luggage. But it does the job for a trip like this. And for a trip like this, I went with my natural inclinations. Throw in everything you might remotely need, right up to the kitchen sink. Jeans, khakis, T-shirts, socks. The black suit I got married in, that went into the garment bag, along with half a dozen good shirts, both dress and casual, black pants, a black sport coat, and a black vest. It got a little bulky, but no big deal. It would all get loaded into the Jeep in the morning.

And that night, it was on my mind pretty strong where I was going. I thought about it. *Here I am, all packed up to hit the road early in the morning. Me and my Jeep are heading up to Aylmer to where Dad is.* These things all jumbled around randomly inside my head. But I knew. I was preparing to walk into a place I had never seen before. Physically, emotionally, spiritually. I could see them in my mind, protruding from the mists, the great dark spires of the castle awaiting my approach.

And somehow, the prayer came to me, in my head. I remembered the stirring majesty of responsive chants echoing through the vast cathedral where I'd attended a Catholic service during my wanderings many years ago. I could hear it in my head like I heard the priest reading and the people responding. Except in this chant, in this prayer, the priest and the people were one and the same. Me, talking to God. *For a calm heart, a clear head, traveling mercies, and strength for the journey, I pray to the Lord. Oh, Lord, hear my prayer.*

I slept fitfully. I usually sleep light when my brain knows there's a full day's travel ahead. That night, I barely dozed off. At one point early in the morning, I woke up and thought, *Maybe I'll just get up and go. Get a good start.* I must have dozed off again, because the next thing I knew, my phone alarm was buzzing at five forty-five a.m. I wanted to be on the road by seven. I shook the cobwebs from my head and got up and showered and dressed. Comfortable clothes. Jeans, a nice checkered shirt, my Danner hikers, and a decently heavy hooded jacket. I was ready. I carried my stuff outside.

I grumbled a good bit at Amish Black, my Jeep, that morning. Those things just don't have a lot of room. And they're hard to load. Why, oh why, didn't I get a four-door while I was at it? Next time, I'll know better. I slid the seat up and swung the heavy suitcase onto the back seat. I had to squash it in back there. Then the garment bag on top, then boxes of this and that. A couple of winter coats, including my Burberry trench. If I was going to a funeral in Canada in late December, there would be some elements of style involved. Didn't matter how full the Jeep got. I may or may not have skinned a knuckle getting everything fitted in. I grumbled some more as I pulled out and headed over to Sheetz for my obligatory coffee. I gassed up, too. And a few minutes before seven, me and Amish Black were heading west on Route 23, on the way out. The little Jeep jitters in and out of traffic like a frightened bug, I'll give it that.

I sipped my Sheetz coffee as we bucketed around Harrisburg and north toward Route 15. And I thought about things as me and my Jeep cruised with the traffic. I had made this trip a lot of times before. Way back in 2012, I think, was one of the first times I drove up to Aylmer to see my parents. Mostly, I went for Mom. She was pretty much out of it with Alzheimer's, and I remembered how it was. How I recoiled from going to see her, or being around her, for a few years there. I turned my face away. But eventually I went. Walked in. Absorbed that what I had been told was true. I was a total stranger to my own mother. There wasn't a glimmer of anything that remotely hinted she knew who I was. It doesn't get much more brutal than that. And I went to see her again the next summer. And then again, before another summer came, this time to her funeral. And then only Dad remained alone.

I thought back through the years and how it felt, driving right down this same road, heading for the same place. And I remembered how I had so desperately longed to reach my father's heart after I left the Amish all those years ago. How I had tried again and again and again. How we simply could not communicate, not outside the boundaries of his world. And it's probably not that he didn't want to, at least I can think that from where I am today. He just didn't know how. I didn't know how, either.

It's a universally powerful thing, the yearning of a child for his father's acceptance and blessing. The heart can be rejected and crushed and rejected and crushed, over and

over, year after year, until that yearning sinks down, somewhere deep inside, and you think it went away. And you
give up. But the seed of that yearning never dies. Not in
the heart. It never dies.

They remain intense in my memories, all those hurts,
the frustrations and bitterness and rage at how it was for
all those long years. And now, this late in Dad's life, something had changed. My father was old, back in those days.
And he had been tired for a long time, really, when I look
back and remember. Sure, he held on to the fire of who he
was for as long as he could grasp it. But with age, a certain
mellowness came seeping in. That's what age does, a lot. It
grinds things down. All the way down to where I went to
see Dad because he wanted me to come. And that was a
strange and wondrous thing, all on its own. That little fact,
right there.

There was a wall there once, a wall of solid rock my
father could never reach through. Now, so late along, now
he wanted me to come, he wanted all of us to come. Now
he wanted to see his children, even the ones who had left
the Amish. Now. And I thought back through all those
years and wondered what it would have been like, had it
always been this way. A lot of turmoil could have been
avoided, and a lot of pain, too. The thing is, it couldn't
have always been this way.

Because it wasn't. Because it all happened as it did.
That's circular reasoning, I know. You hold on to what you
can grasp, when you look back at things that were, things
that can never be changed. It couldn't have been different,
because it wasn't. The wall was what it was. There are a lot

of old wounds buried in the rubble of that wall. And not just mine. They are the wounds of all his children. But that wall couldn't have come down any other way, I don't think. No other way than age and time. That's how I look at it. It couldn't have, because it didn't.

And it's hard sometimes, in your heart, to let the hard things go. But when there's no other better choice, you have to. For your own sanity, you have to.

Such were my thoughts as I drove this same road many times over the years to see Dad. That was my reason for going, each time. And we went to a few places we hadn't been before, me and my father. We got some things hashed out, or at least discussed. As old as he was, I figured he probably wouldn't remember much of what we had talked about for long. But we talked about those things, such as they were, in the moment. I told him some stuff I never figured could ever be said. And he talked to me honestly, like he never had back when I was growing up around him. I am beyond grateful that the opportunity came and that we both took it. And every time I left, I thought this might well be the last trip like this. It never was. He always fought hard to stay alive and stay alert. It was a matter of some pride to him that he had lasted more years than any of his siblings. Not that it makes any difference in the end. Ashes to ashes, and dust to dust, like the preacher says. All that is true.

And now. Now I was going to see him again. Maybe this would be the last such drive north. I didn't know, that day. And I didn't fret about it. I did think about it, driving along. What should I be focused on as I'm going up to see my dying father? I mean, surely there are profound things a son would naturally mull over in a time like that. I remember thinking, *The primary thing you focus on right now is the road. Keep your mind sharp on that. It won't do you any good to go see Dad if you don't get there.* And I thought, too, *God, I know Dad's suffering. I ask you to take him, even right now, this minute. I'm completely at peace if he leaves before I get there. So feel free. I mean, you are God. Take my father home.*

PAST

I LEFT THE Amish a long time ago. More than half my lifetime. I was twenty-six, going on twenty-seven. And this is how it was, how I felt. They were my people, the Amish, and they would always be, but I could not abide with them. I could not live that way. It was too hard, too maddening. And there had been a long slog over a lot of broken roads before I figured out that I could leave and not be lost. When that truth sank in, I was done. Never again would I wander as lonely or as far as I did back in those years of running and searching. I could almost get nostalgic about it. But nah. I was tired, and I was done.

I thought back on it a lot of times. Now and then, I tried to see it all from the perspective of my parents. How did they feel when I walked away? After all those years and times I returned once more? Then I settled in again and walked right up to the door of marrying Sarah, the beautiful Amish girl. After all that, I turned my back and threw it all away? How did they feel, watching that happen? It had to be hard on them. Both Dad and Mom. It had to be. And looking back at it from here, it seemed like Dad was always opining and admonishing. Mom was quiet. Her silence spoke her pain. She smiled, real enough. But she knew what suffering was. And she knew what loss was, too. The men in her family saw to that, her husband and her sons.

So there they were, my parents, back there when I left for good. There they were, in an awkward place. Wherever he lived, Dad was always a pillar of the Amish community. He was a pillar in the larger Amish world, too. So well known, so widely read, so hugely respected. And here one more of his whacked-out sons went haywire. Threw everything to the winds and ran. People clucked and said what they had said for years: "David Wagler has wild sons. Can't control them." It had to be a bitter pill. He kept walking, though, as he knew how.

I remember him talking about Sarah, the beautiful Amish girl I had left behind. Dad had always liked Sarah a lot. He had a special place in his heart for her. Mom did, too. They both looked on her almost as a daughter. Which she came pretty close to being at one point there, I guess. They never could quite let it go, my parents, their visions of what might have been. This is simply an observation, not a judgment. It was what it was. As life mostly is.

I remember Dad telling me, "You wronged that woman. And you will pay for it one day. You can't treat someone like that, so it doesn't come back at you. You will pay." I just stared at him. Outwardly, of course, I shrugged. So what if I had to pay? I probably needed to, in some way. But that's still better than it would have been, had I stayed. That would have been disaster. I'm glad I didn't see the mess life would have been, had I not left when I did.

Still. I never forgot my father's warning, so flatly spoken. What goes around comes around. And I think Dad might have smiled secretly to himself a few times in the years that followed. His words turned out to be prophetic, probably way sooner than he'd ever expected. Straight and true like an arrow, his words were. I did pay for how I treated Sarah. Multiple times on multiple levels, I'd say. The old man knew what he was talking about on that one. Of course, those things always look a lot bigger in the moment, when they're coming at you. In retrospect, after the passing of years, it all levels out a little. And you realize a lot of that hard stuff from way back when, a lot of that was just life. Other people go through things like that, too, maybe way harder things than you did. It's a little unsettling when that raw little truth comes knocking on the door.

It took long enough to hit me. I certainly had little grasp of what it all meant back when Dad warned me I would pay for how I had treated Sarah. This was right at the time I was settling into my post-Amish world. Back in Daviess. That was where I headed instinctively. I didn't have a lot of connections anywhere. No real network of any kind. So I went to the land that harbored the roots of my family from both sides. And Daviess welcomed me.

It's hard, remembering after all these years. What it felt like to walk from my Amish world into an English one. Well, at the beginning of my new life, there were some remnants of Plainness among the Mennonites. The Plain Mennonites were a stepping stone, pretty much. But they treated me with kindness and respect. Overall, I have good memories of the Mennonites and Daviess. It was a new place with new dimensions, my post-Amish world.

In such a world, you get to go buy yourself a car.

The year was 1988. I had saved a decent stake from working in the factories in northern Indiana, a stash of $9,000. It seemed like a small fortune, more money than I had ever seen before at one time. I took half of that and bought an ugly tan-gold T-Bird, a 1984 model, if I remember the year right. Me and that old T-Bird traveled tens of thousands of miles on the open road and saw a lot of life together over the next few years.

I worked construction in Daviess right after I got there. That was about the only real marketable skill I had. My pay was next to nothing. I boarded in a little trailer house owned by my Wagler friends, the family that had taken me in years ago when a lot of turmoil was going on around me. They were distant relatives, Dean and his brothers. The trailer house was set up nicely on one of their turkey farms. And I settled into my move from the Amish world into a modern world.

On Sundays I went to Mount Olive Mennonite Church. They had a few habits that I wasn't used to. Most notably, they had church services on Wednesday nights as well as Sunday mornings. Wednesday-night prayer meeting. Sitting in church had never been on my list of favorite activities. Attending an Amish church service meant sitting on a hard bench for a long time. Your back got tired, and you might or might not hear something you would actually remember from the sermon.

Mount Olive is a pretty strict place. Lots of grim-faced men peered around suspiciously to make sure nobody was having too much fun. Life was serious. Our somber faces must always reflect some degree of awareness of that fact. Too much smiling was unseemly and ultimately sinful. It reminded me a little bit of the old Aylmer people, way back in my childhood, how humorless they had been.

I remember my first Wednesday-night service at Mount Olive. I wasn't used to going to church during the week. But I was told that was how the Mennonites did it. And seeing how I was fixing to join the Mennonites, I might as well get used to it. (I never did.) The prayer meeting was kind of like a Bible study, really, except it was the whole church. Someone had a topic of some sort. The topics were short sermons and were usually dry as a bone. There was a lot of admonishing going on, about what it meant to live right. And lots of *Amens*. After the topic that first night, we split off into small groups. I tagged along with the little group of youth as we walked down to the basement. We sat in a circle, and someone asked for prayer requests. People said things like "We need rain. Crops are real dry." Or "Let's pray for so-and-so, that he'll get saved." I can't remember a personal, vulnerable request ever coming from anyone. Judgment would have been too harsh.

That Wednesday, after the requests were gathered, someone started praying. A short prayer, maybe a minute or two. Then the next person in the circle prayed. I stirred and looked around in panic. The prayers were creeping right around the circle, and soon it would be my turn. I had never prayed aloud in public. I didn't know how. What should I say? The guy next to me was taking his turn. He prayed, and then it was my turn.

I remember that time only because of that frozen moment. I sat there, silent and paralyzed. I couldn't speak. After an agonizing five or ten seconds, I waved my hand. I pass. And mercifully, the guy on the other side of me didn't hesitate. He prayed his little prayer. And it went on around the circle until it was finished. Nobody mentioned anything about how I had not prayed. But I felt pretty ashamed. At the next prayer meeting, I managed to squeak out a few words. It was hard to force myself. I just didn't come from a place like that. In time, I got to be decently fluent in speaking aloud to the Lord. But my spoken prayers were never long. They still aren't. Not anything like the unspoken prayers in my heart. Those prayers go on and on, every day, like a preacher who doesn't know when it's time to shut up and sit down. I'm OK with that, though. I think the Lord is OK with that, too.

DAVIESS AND
VINCENNES

I'M A GLUTTON for tough times and hard roads, seems like. And the winter of 1988–1989 was tough for me in many ways, which isn't that surprising. This was just one more struggle in a long string of struggles.

There wasn't a lot of support around me as I settled into my post-Amish world in Daviess. And always, it seemed, something hard rose to confront me. That winter, I was reeling from the abrupt loss of a relationship I had desperately wished would work out. It did not. Instead, it collapsed into dust and ashes around me, because I could not speak my heart.

I hunched down and absorbed the bitter pain of a loss such as I had never known. Dad's little prophecy came true, what he'd spoken about me paying for how I had treated Sarah. Did it ever. Still. It was probably more intense in my mind because of how alone I felt. And how alone I was in my new world, my new life in Daviess. It's not like I could communicate much, not like I could really trust anyone around me, to talk to. Mostly because I didn't know how. And somewhere, in the spasms of that pain, the shadows of a plan came to my mind. Leave this behind. Strike out into a new place. Get my GED, the equivalent of a high school diploma. Get that, and maybe enroll at Indiana's Vincennes University in the fall.

I wasn't sure just what all was involved. At twenty-seven, I had a limited education. I couldn't imagine taking the tests for my GED without some preparation. So I made some calls. There were classes one could take at a local school in Washington, Indiana. Tuesday nights, if I remember right. And a week or so later, I walked in and enrolled. Tentatively, a bit scared. I don't remember the nice lady's name, but I remember how helpful she was. "Oh, yes," she said. "Yes, yes. Come on in. We'll analyze where you are. Take some placement exams. We'll figure out what you need to learn. And we'll teach you what you don't know, so you can get your GED. And go on to college. Don't be afraid. You can do this."

Grateful for her words, I took the placement exams. And amazingly, in pretty much every category, I was already at college entry level. Except one. Math. I had a strong but basic eighth-grade education from the Aylmer Amish school. Since then, I had devoured countless books. I had read and read and read. Much trash. And some good stuff, too. But who goes out and learns math on their own? A math brain, I guess. Definitely not me. Still, I was astounded and emboldened. I could do this. And I began attending classes, there in Washington, to learn some basic elements of math. And to polish up my writing.

And after a couple of months of attending those weekly classes, I took the plunge. Went in and sat for my GED tests. I don't recall many specific details of that day, except I was fairly confident. And when my scores came back, they were good. Actually, in a very high percentile. The nice lady smiled and congratulated me. She knew I could do it. This is the beginning. Now go enroll at Vincennes. Here's all the information you need to do that. And I did. Enrolled at a real university, for the fall of 1989. I was excited. This was a new road, a new day. I knew what was behind me, I'd just walked from there. There was no way I could possibly envision what waited ahead for me.

Three days before my twenty-eighth birthday. That's when I walked through the doors of Vincennes University as a student for the first time. Clutching my new bright-blue JanSport backpack loaded with textbooks, I entered the halls of the Humanities Building. That's the stuff I had signed up for, mostly. English. Literature. History. Speech. And one lone remedial math class, way across the campus.

It was a magical and frightening time. Magical because of the new possibilities that so suddenly seemed within my grasp. And frightening because of where I'd come from. I was a simple ex-Amish man, with not a day of high school under my belt. That's intimidating, any way you look at it. And yet here it was before me. All I had to do was walk forward through the open door. College. The real thing. A world that called to a deep place in my heart. And to me, it was pretty much a miracle, this university. Vincennes University. A two-year school. The gateway to my journey through a world I had never dared to imagine.

I lapped it up from the first day. Timidly, I took a seat in my first class. Way in the back of the room, which would forever after be my most comfortable spot. World Literature, with Dr. Rodgers. A frail little wisp of a man, not that well-spoken. But very knowledgeable. He hemmed and hawed and welcomed us. This semester, we will be exploring this theme and that theme in our studies. We'll be writing a paper every month. The syllabus described our course. Syllabus? What was that? I had never heard that word before. Had no clue what it meant.

I would soon hear a lot of words that I had never heard spoken before. Words I had read, words the meaning of which I knew full well. But there's a difference between reading a word and hearing it used in actual conversations, properly articulated. I cringed at the way I'd been pronouncing some of them. And I listened and learned.

That first semester, I signed up for what was considered a full load. Fifteen hours. English I. History of some kind. Literature. And a few other classes I can't recall. But it was the humanities—the reading, the writing, that side of the brain—that was my strength. And I walked naturally through those doors, which seemed to call my name. I was new there. Didn't know whom or what I could trust. So I went by instinct.

And to me, it was like a smorgasbord, the university. It was as if I were seated at a table groaning under the weight of a great feast of so many mysteries I longed to touch and taste. And feel. I eagerly read the assigned literature. Completed the writings on time. I was serious, focused, and hungry, and that was soon plain to those around me.

Within a month, all my professors knew my name, knew who I was. And to their credit, every single one of them acknowledged and welcomed this student who had emerged from the backwoods of the "peaceful people," the Amish. Every single one. Their doors were always open to me, and I soon felt calm and comfortable enough to just stop by and chat. To talk of things. To pick their brains. I was right at ten years older than the average college freshman. I'd lived ten tough years of life most of my classmates had never seen and probably would never see. And to me, it was a huge privilege just to be there at this formal place where knowledge was the market.

After that first semester, fifteen credit hours were not enough to occupy my mind. The second semester, I took eighteen hours. And in my second year at Vincennes, on a full merit scholarship, I enrolled in twenty-one class hours both semesters. Sure, this was a junior college. Not a four-year school. Not as rigorous. But for me, well, I could not have found a more perfect launching place. Vincennes University was a shining city on a hill.

Those were glorious days of high adventure. I felt like I was on a mountain, looking out over the vast expanses of fertile valleys below. This, this was the journey I had been searching for, without even knowing. Somehow, I recognized that.

I rented a room to stay in, a few miles from the college. An attic bedroom. I think I paid $150 a month. And I worked, too.

Right then, Daviess County was buzzing with a great deal of gossip and speculation. A group of visionary investors had just opened a huge new restaurant complex on the outskirts of Montgomery, Indiana. Named The Gasthof, it featured Amish-style cooking and had a large gift shop. One of my friends told me they were still hiring servers. I'd often considered waiting on tables. The classic job for a student: you worked, you got your tips, and you got money to live on. Now, as a full-time student, I definitely needed some cash flow. I decided to apply.

I walked in one afternoon. The place was simply breath-taking in its vastness. Rough timber framing with wooden pegs. Post and beam throughout. Seating space for several hundred diners. Two banquet rooms, including one on the second floor. And the gift shop. After ogling the place, I inquired about a job and met with Gene and Mabel Bon-trager, the managers. We hit it off right away. I was hired on the spot for Friday and Saturday evenings. They told me to wear a white shirt and black pants and black shoes. And to come Tuesday evening for training and orientation. Half the minimum hourly wage plus tips. And so began my career as a waiter, one that would last through four years of college.

At The Gasthof, I usually arrived and clocked in at four o'clock in the afternoon. The place closed at nine. During the first hour or so, things were usually slow. We paced nervously. Where were the customers? We needed work. And tips. Around five o'clock, the floodgates opened. Suddenly the place was swarming. No more nervous pacing. Hammer down, all night. The next four hours were a frantic race to keep up, to feed as many people as possible and get them back out the door, fat and happy.

I could never figure out where all the people came from. This wasn't Lancaster County. Not that there was much time to mull over such esoteric questions. A typical waiter or waitress was responsible for five to seven tables. I took to the work quite naturally, and a good night netted anywhere from $80 to $110 in tips. For four or five hours of work, that wasn't a bad wage. Especially back in 1989.

A server has one responsibility. Make the dining experience as relaxed and enjoyable as possible for the customer. And as smooth as possible. The better you can do that, the better the tip. Well, not always, but as a rule. Be unobtrusive but available. Does the customer want conversation? If so, chat a bit. If not, fade back and respect privacy. Don't interrupt too often. Keep your eyes on your customers. I often stood leaning against a wall, seemingly doing nothing, but scanning my tables constantly for the slightest sign a customer needed something. And I responded instantly when they did. Refilled drinks and coffee without being asked. Removed dishes when done. Smiled, regardless of the situation, no matter how rude the customer. Thanked them when they were leaving. Invited them back. Picked up the tip they left, and slipped it into my apron. I was always aware. Don't act too eager picking up those bills. Your other customers are watching.

At The Gasthof, the servers developed a real rapport with each other. There were a few other male servers, but most were high school and college girls. I listened to more dating problems and discussions about guys (from the girls' perspectives) than I could have imagined possible. Break-ups. Pursuits. Fights. I heard it all in excruciating detail. By remaining quiet and emitting an occasional sympathetic grunt, I soon developed a reputation of being quite wise. And so I heard even more problems. A sympathetic ear with an occasional sympathetic grunt multiplies exponentially what you hear, believe me. But it was all good. The experience, I mean. Not the problems. After hours, we'd often go out for pizza or meet at someone's house just to hang out. And swap tales from the battlefield.

And looking back at those times of hanging out, I will say this. Kids are kids, wherever they are. Amish or English. You hang out. You have fun. You talk about your world. Whatever world that is.

The Gasthof had many Amish workers and servers. And many Amish customers. At that time, most local Amish customers did not tip. They still don't, in the more backward communities, because they don't know enough to do so. I hang my head now in shame and remember the dozens and dozens of servers I stiffed over the years when I was Amish. I simply didn't know. And once I learned, it was like getting clobbered over the head by a two-by-four. *Oh, good grief,* I thought. *How naive could I possibly have been for all those years?* The thing is, you don't know what you don't know until you do know. And no one can dictate when that time gets here.

If you got a table full of Amish, you simply counted it as a loss, when it came to tips. And told the hostess you'd had your turn in the rotation. Once, for breakfast, a waitress served a table of ten or so Amish customers. As they were leaving, she saw no one had left anything. Then one little old Amish man came limping back, beaming, and thanked her for her service. She held her breath. Would this be the exception? With a grand flourish, he handed her a quarter. Beaming with goodwill. She stammered an astounded thank-you. It was not an insult. They simply didn't know to tip. They paid for the food and probably felt that was costly enough. But that was years ago. It may be different now, at least in the more progressive Amish settlements.

One busy Saturday evening, the hostess hunted me down in a panic. She pointed out a trio of sour old ladies who had been overlooked unintentionally for more than half an hour. They were mad. And the waitress who was responsible for that table was afraid to approach them. Would I serve them? What could I say? Sure. I approached. They sat stonily like a trio of grim judges. I apologized for the delay and asked if they were ready for some good food.

"We don't know if it will be good," the oldest one snapped. She was rotund and wore wire-rimmed glasses. "We haven't tasted the food yet and the service so far has been terrible." The others sniffed in disdainful agreement.

Undeterred, young, idealistic, and full of energy and goodwill that would be difficult to dredge up now, I decided to accept their outraged grumpiness as a personal challenge. And so I gave them the most perfect service of which I was capable. Even though the evening was extremely busy, I made sure their drinks were always filled. The food served hot. I gave them free desserts. Slowly they softened. The grumpiest old lady, the one with the wire-rimmed glasses, even smiled a time or two. After they left, the waitress who was originally supposed to serve them almost collapsed in gratitude. She came and hugged me hard. And I found two shiny quarters on the table. I consider that tip among my most memorable ever. From an insurmountable negative to a positive two quarters. You take what you can get.

And soon enough, I got through my first semester. Then my first year. My confidence grew exponentially, almost weekly. I soon knew I could conquer whatever this journey brought my way. It was the first time ever, in my life, that I had been exposed to people and surroundings from such a broad spectrum. Yeah, Vincennes was pretty much a local college. But it was still a new and exciting experience for me, simply because the world I had come from was so vastly, vastly limited. And here I was, venturing way out there into strange new lands such as my people had never known or seen before. Not the people from my world, in the past.

That first year, Dr. Bernard Verkamp, my philosophy teacher and good friend, got me to apply for a full scholarship for my second and final year at Vincennes. The Galligan Scholarship in Philosophy. I remember that name because the plaque they gave me hangs on the wall beside my desk. I never framed any diploma I ever got from anywhere. Except the honorary doctorate of letters Vincennes awarded me after my first book got published. That hangs on the wall by my desk, because that thing came framed. And that's the only reason it's hanging anywhere.

Back then, I did what Dr. Verkamp told me to. Filled out an application. I wrote a little essay about what education, and philosophy in particular, meant to me. Of course, I mentioned my background a few times in the essay. I come from the Amish. From the backcountry. I never had a day of high school. And now I'm at your college. I mean, am I dreaming, or what? And oh yeah, I really enjoy and value my philosophy classes, too. Which was not a lie. I enjoyed Dr. Verkamp's classes immensely. I enrolled in one of his classes every semester I was there.

There was an interview, too, that I had to do with the scholarship board. I was very relaxed, and the board seemed impressed when I left. Dr. Verkamp confidently told me I should be a shoo-in.

And I remember, too, how I bragged a little the next time I saw my father. That first summer after the first year at VU. I remember that he asked all about my college classes. Once, I took home a few of my handwritten essays that had been turned in, graded, and returned to me. Dad took them and read them. He seemed impressed. This was a real essay that had been submitted in a real college. He asked a lot of questions about what I was studying and such. And after that first year, that summer, I told him the news. I got a full scholarship for next year for college. He asked about it. And he laughed almost before he could catch himself. Saving all the money on tuition, that made sense to him. He seemed a little proud. Or maybe I was just imagining.

And it seems so strange, looking back. Strange how deeply I craved the man's approval. I knew he could never really come out and say it, that he was proud. And I knew that when I came around, there would be at least one obligatory admonition. The usual stuff he always dredged up from somewhere. From what his father had told him, maybe, long before. I don't know. But it was always the same, what he spoke. "Me and Mom feel that you should just come back and make your things right and be Amish. You really have no need to go to college. What good is that going to do you?" The man persisted in this singular message for more than a decade after I left, after he knew there was no way I would ever return. He still spoke those rote words, I guess because he thought he had to. Or at least that he should.

The second year at Vincennes rolled by. Sometime that fall, I think it was, Dr. Verkamp asked me for my father's address. He wanted to write a letter. I never poked around much as to what he meant to tell Dad. But Dad sure told me what Dr. Verkamp had written him, the next time I went home. And Dad actually beamed as he showed me the letter. My philosopher friend had been most gracious. He'd told Dad that I was among the very best and brightest students he had ever taught at the college level. I felt some pride when Dad told me that.

My relationships with all my professor friends deepened. I was probably a little selfish, but they didn't seem to mind when I stopped by their offices to just talk about whatever. My brain was open, and my mind was hungry. I had always read a lot. I mean, Dad always had a lot of books around. But there was never any real place to talk to others about what you were reading, not in any structured way. And these professors had a trove of accumulated knowledge that I wanted to grasp as my own. They heard and absorbed my excited questions, saw my hungry eyes. And they spoke to me as an equal, almost. Intellectually, I mean.

Dr. Phillip E. Pierpont, the dean of humanities, seemed

like a stuffed shirt the first time I saw him. Formal, mannered, pompous, impeccably dressed in suit and tie. And then I took his class. It must have been Classical Literature, because I remember reading portions of *The Iliad* and *The Odyssey*. Dr. Pierpont knew his stuff. The man was a fantastic teacher. Always formally dressed in suit and tie. He was known to give hard tests. I was so engrossed that I barely noticed. I knew the answers because I was keenly interested in the subject matter. I stopped by his office regularly and got to know his staff quite well. Dr. Pierpont had three lovely assistants. They always greeted me cheerfully. Of course, I bantered right back. I even had my own chair, which someone labeled with my name on the bottom of the frame.

Dr. Pierpont advised me, both as a professional and as a friend. And he was determined that I should apply at Notre Dame. He was a devout Catholic, and Notre Dame was about as big a thing as he could imagine for me. He even wrote a lengthy letter of recommendation. I was touched and honored. But I wasn't sure. Notre Dame? That sounded a little out there. I still wasn't far enough beyond where I'd come from to trust myself in such a secular setting. And yeah, I know. Notre Dame is a religious school. But to someone who came from the Amish, that place was a vast and darkly gleaming city of secular academics and worldliness.

"I just don't know," I told Dr. Pierpont. "I think I need something a bit more structured." From my plain Mennonite circles, I had heard the name of another school. Another college. Down south a ways. Bob Jones University.

I'm sure Dr. Pierpont was horrified when I told him. He had to be. I had just emerged from Hickville, and now I was deliberately walking back in. That's what he thought, I always figured later. But his training kicked in. Formal and mannerly is what he was. So he never let on. Through all my days at Vincennes and during my later transfer to Bob Jones, my good friend Dr. Pierpont enthusiastically supported me in any way he could. He was a kind and decent man.

In the spring of 1991, a new day approached for me. Graduation. I was marching summa cum laude with an Associate's Degree in General Studies. I guess that degree and fifty cents (at that time) would have bought me a cup of coffee. But still. I was excited and eager. This was a big deal for me. And back in Daviess, I told my friends, "I'm graduating." I told my family too, the Amish ones in Bloomfield, Iowa, and the others where they were scattered. "I'm graduating." Not that I expected anyone to show up, really. But I still wanted to share my good news in my world. I'm graduating from Vincennes University.

I didn't make a big fuss about the graduation. But still. You invite your people.

Graduation day came. In gown and mortarboard tasseled cap, I proudly marched across the stage. Received my diploma. Somewhere, there is a faded picture of me standing there on the stage, shaking the hand of whoever was president at Vincennes back then. I was smiling and clutching my diploma.

The first in my family to even remotely dream of such a thing, let alone do it, I knew before I marched. But I looked out over the audience anyway. Other than my professors and a few dozen staff and students I had befriended at the university, not a single friend or family member was present to cheer my accomplishment.

Not one.

For me, it didn't seem like that big a deal at the moment. And it didn't really bug me that much. It was corn-planting time in Daviess. My local friends were in the fields and all. Working twenty-hour days, getting the crops in. They begged off, but you do what you have to do. I came from the Amish. Of course I understood. The farm work comes first. Only years later did it hit me how fragile my support structure was at that time. And there was little semblance of a safety net at all.

It was what it was. And I'm just saying how it was.

In the years that passed, I vowed to myself that if any of my nephews or nieces or siblings ever graduated with any kind of post-high-school degree, anywhere, I would make every effort to attend if it was remotely feasible. And I have. Mostly.

SUMMER IN LANCASTER

I LIVE IN Lancaster County. Smack-dab in the heart of one of the largest Amish communities in the world. Not to mention the oldest. And coming from where I've been, I sometimes feel like the odd man out here, drifting in a sea of cultural blue bloods.

And yes, one might well ask, Lancaster County—what's up with that? Did the guy ever really leave the Amish, as he claims? Why can't he seem to shake them for good?

Well, yes, I left. For good, as I wrote at the end of my first book. I never returned to Bloomfield, Iowa, where most of my Rumspringa unfolded. Or to Goshen, Indiana, which is the last place on earth where I ever was Amish. I never went back to either of those places, except to visit. But never to try again. I made my final departure. At that time, roughly the spring of 1988, there was little about the culture that attracted me. I wanted to shake it all off, the last vestiges of those chains. I was free at last. After all those years of turmoil. Free. And it felt great.

And yeah, there was some resentment bubbling inside me. A little bit of anger. I didn't wear it on my sleeve, but it was there inside my heart. And I spoke it now and then. These people were stuck in their backward ways. They were welcome to stay there. The memories were still so raw inside and so fresh. I was done. Gone. For good. I would never look back, except in gratitude that I had finally escaped. That's how I felt.

Back when I'd first enrolled at Vincennes, in the summer of 1989, before my first fall semester, I came to Lancaster County. Not out of curiosity, but for strictly economic reasons. I needed money for college. I had a connection in Lancaster, a good friend. And he told me, Come on in. Wages are way higher. You can make some real money here. More than you ever will in Daviess. Come on in. And the decision was easy. I had been a rolling stone for most of my adult life. So it seemed like a good idea, to roll on some more. Lancaster. I'd heard so much about the place. I remembered how odd they had seemed, the people from there, way back when they'd visited us in Aylmer.

And so in May of that year, I loaded my ugly tan-gold T-Bird and headed east. Arrived in Lancaster safely. It's a beautiful area. Old, for this country. Lots of history. Tiny narrow ribbons of paved roads wind and twist through the countryside. Countless tidy little farms are dotted about. Ancient stone houses and great red barns, owned by the same families for generations. Real roots, here. None of the vagabonding like my father had done decades ago. These people were planted here. Born here. Lived here. Died here.

And the strange Amish buggies with rounded tops and straight sides practically clogged the roads, hitched to wild, high-stepping horses. You couldn't have paid me to ride those buggies on those roads. Still couldn't. I almost felt like a tourist, seeing this brand of Amish for the first time.

And that summer was a time of labor and sweat. I worked long, hard hours five days a week, sometimes six. I wanted to work to save. And I wanted to work to forget. I used those long, hard days to leave behind what was lost and to lay up for the future. And those three months were amazing, looking back. But I didn't meet a whole lot of Amish people. I had no desire to, really. Sure, I said hi when passing in the regular stream of commerce. Mostly, I hung out with the Beachy Amish youth at Pequea Church. They were friendly and accepting, welcomed me. Invited me to their social activities. It was a good summer, and a short one. In August, I left for Daviess and Vincennes, still convinced that the Lancaster Old Order Amish were one strange bunch.

The next summer I returned to Lancaster. And again, I made no attempt to meet any Amish people or get to know them. Still wanted nothing to do with them. The summer passed, and I returned to Daviess and my second and final year at Vincennes.

The third summer, after graduating from Vincennes, that's when things started shaking. And changing. I boarded with Ben and Emma Stoltzfus and their family. On their farm just east of Honey Brook, over the line in Chester County. Upstairs, in the third-floor attic of the farmhouse. A cozy little place that would be my Pennsylvania home base for about the next five years. Beachy Amish people who drove cars, Ben and Emma became as close to my surrogate parents as any couple ever has. I treasure the memories of their kindness. And their love.

And one summer evening, after I'd returned from a long day of working in the sun, Emma had a message for me. Some Amish guy had called that day. Elmer. Asked lots of questions. Was I staying there? Was I David Wagler's son? Emma had told him yes and promised she would tell me. And she did. I was supposed to call him back. She gave me the number to his phone shack, which was where the Lancaster Amish had their phones back then. In a little shack, off on its own outside somewhere. Just as long as it wasn't too handy.

I looked at the slip of paper and shrugged. This was about the last thing I needed, some Amish guy tracking me down. I had just broken away a few short years back. I knew plenty of Amish people, even a few I still considered my friends. Why would I want to get to know any more? I pitched the number. Didn't return Elmer's call. He'd go away if I ignored him, I figured. Another nosy Amish man with all kinds of invasive questions. No way, I wasn't playing that game. He probably wanted to admonish me for leaving. Tell me to go back, to "straighten up and settle down" where I should be, back in Bloomfield, Iowa, where my family was. The place I had fled. I didn't want to hear it. Not this time. That song had been played too many times. No more, I would listen to it no more.

And a week or so later, another message. Emma smiled almost apologetically and told me as I walked in, exhausted, from a hard day's work. Elmer had called again. Insisted that he wanted to see me. Again, I shrugged. Who was this wacko Amish man? So persistent. Well, I could be persistent, too. And again, I pitched the phone-shack number. Ignored the man.

And then Elmer unlimbered the big guns. He didn't call Emma again. Oh, no. He waited, craftily, until evening the next time he called, about a week later. I don't remember who answered the phone. But it was for me. It was Elmer. The Amish guy.

I gave up right then. Any man that persistent at least deserved an answer directly from me. So I walked into the front room, kind of a parlor. Took the phone. "Hello."

And a calm, pleasant voice spoke. Precisely stating the words. "Good evening. This is Elmer. Is this Ira?"

"Yes, it is." A few brief polite pleasantries.

"Hey, would you stop by some Saturday soon? We would love to meet you, my wife and I."

And there I stood, stuck. No. I don't want to meet you. No. I don't need to be admonished by any new Amish "friends." But I couldn't just say that. Too rude. So I hedged. "Yeah, that might work. What did you have in mind?" Of course, the following Saturday afternoon suited Elmer just fine. And, of course, I had nothing else planned. So, reluctantly, I agreed. "Where do you live?"

"It's simple," Elmer claimed. "We live just off the highway." And he gave me specific directions.

"OK," I promised. "I'll be there this Saturday afternoon."

"I look forward to meeting you," he said.

I mumbled something incoherent in response. We hung up.

That Saturday afternoon, I headed out shortly after one. In my old T-Bird. It's hard to describe just how ugly that car was. Not the shape, necessarily. But the color. Tan gold. It was just gag-me awful. I haven't owned that many vehicles in my lifetime, but I have owned two of the ugliest colors in the spectrum. The old avocado-green Dodge. And that awful tan-gold T-Bird. Other than the color, though, the T-Bird was a decent car. It got me to where I was going, for a good many years. As a destitute student. So I guess I should honor it a little more.

I drove down the crowded two-lane highway toward Lancaster. Turned right onto Elmer's road. A mile or two in, then I turned into his drive. Nice place. Clean as a whistle, like most Amish places in Lancaster County. Not even a wayward leaf on the ground anywhere. Neat freaks, like all Lancaster Amish people. I parked. Got out and walked toward the house. Strangely, I wasn't particularly nervous. This meeting was coming down, and it would be what it would be.

Elmer met me at the door. We shook hands and introduced ourselves. Then he welcomed me into his home. I walked in. Met his smiling wife, Naomi, and their clan of quiet children. All of them milled about. I scanned the room, amazed. Stacks of books were strewn about everywhere. Not fluff books, either. Literature. Theology. Bestsellers. I was instantly impressed. And as I looked into their faces, I suddenly knew that they were genuinely happy that I was there, in their home. It wasn't just their smiles. It was their eyes. There was no hint of judgment in them. None. Nothing but pure honest joyful welcome. I didn't know such a thing even existed in the Amish world.

And that was my first taste of how it can be, and how it could have been so much earlier in my world. To be accepted as I was, for who I was, by someone from my background, my culture. Truly accepted. And truly welcomed. There was not a shade of a cloud of any reservation. None. I don't think I could quite grasp, quite wrap my head around what that meant to me in that moment.

I won't claim that I was suddenly magically relieved of my resentment toward the Amish in general right then. I wasn't. I won't claim that I decided right then that Lancaster County would be my future home. I didn't. I was a rolling stone. Heading off to Bob Jones University in South Carolina that fall. I had no idea where I'd end up. I didn't think ahead that much. I was focused only on working summers to earn enough to survive another year of college without loading up on too much crushing debt. I'd settle where I'd settle, when the time came.

I will say that when I met Elmer and his family, that was my first real taste of people from my culture who embraced me, even though I had chosen to walk away. And that was a profound and startling thing to me. A minor miracle. To realize that such people could exist. I thought I knew the Amish as a group, and all their mind-sets. I didn't. Because I had never been exposed to certain elements of the Lancaster County Amish before.

The blue bloods came through. That's all I can say. They

fully deserve the status they claim for themselves. They are the real thing. What the Amish could be and should be.

That said, they're not all like Elmer and his family, the Lancaster Amish. Not nearly all. Even here, most are more like the type of Amish I knew growing up. Especially down south. South-enders, we call them. They tend to be a little more hard-core, a little more Plain. I can usually tell when I meet them. Who they are and what they are. By how they look. I can sense their spirit. And tell who they are from certain shadows in their eyes.

That was many years ago, when Elmer finagled me into coming to his home. After that first time, the place became a regular Saturday-afternoon stop for me. I soon developed a deep, quiet friendship with the whole family. Off and on, I've been there, a character in their lives as the children grew into adults. Married now, almost all of them, with children of their own. There were a few stretches through the years when I lost contact for a while, but I always circled back. Back to a zone of comfort that welcomed me, that offered shelter from the storms. Back to real true friends.

And in time, my mind relaxed as well. My journey looped back, back to my roots. And I settled in where there was comfort and support. I will never be accepted as a true Lancastrian. No one not born here is. But I'm settled, in my head. This is my home. Today, some of my closest friends are Old Order Amish. Right here around me in Lancaster County.

It might make sense, or it might make no sense, to those who have broken away from restrictive religious backgrounds. That I hang so close to the culture that caused so much pain. It might be mostly an Amish thing, I don't know. Years ago, my oldest brother, Joseph, was traveling by bus somewhere through Texas. At the bus station in some big city, a guy walked up to him. Completely English. Spoke to him in broken Pennsylvania Dutch. He had left the culture decades before. Lost pretty much all contact with his roots. And sometimes he randomly drove over to the bus station just to see if some Amish people might be passing through. And that day, Joseph was. They visited for a while, and the guy left. Still then, years later, he could not deny his longing for some connection to his culture. Something in his heart moved him to do what he did. There is no way to really disconnect, however much one might want to.

I chose to circle back, to live among them, the Amish. I could have chosen not to, and that would have been perfectly OK as well. I certainly don't live like them or follow their lifestyle. Couldn't do that if I tried. And I have no desire to. When I go "home" to visit, I stay in a motel. Because after spending the day in what used to be my world, I'm always quite ready to return to modern conveniences.

My people and my culture will always be a part of my identity. Will always be a part of who I am, how I react, how I see things. And nothing will ever change that fact. I can deny it. Or accept it. Either way, it's still true.

It's important to face and make peace with the past. And all it ever was, good or bad. Whatever the flaws of those in that world, to accept them. Whatever the hurts, to forgive those who inflicted them. Whatever the wounds, to seek healing. Which can be no small thing, sometimes, I know well enough. It wasn't a small thing for me, and my journey was a walk in the park compared to that of those who have endured and survived every imaginable form of abuse. But it can be done, and it must be done. For a whole lot of good reasons. But mostly, for the sake of your own heart.

Because a heart that refuses to be healed will never be truly free.

BOB JONES
UNIVERSITY

IN 1991, I packed up all my earthly possessions, which consisted of a fairly meager little pile. A sparse assortment of clothes, including a few dress pants, jeans, a few dress shirts, and a couple of suits. And a couple of boxes holding a decent collection of books. And many boxes of odds and ends, the dust of living. More than enough to fill a car. And I loaded all my stuff into my ugly tan-gold T-Bird. I felt it in my head and heart, the loss of leaving the familiar. But I had accomplished all I could here. It was time to leave the land that had been my home for the past three years, aside from summers. Daviess.

I sensed it would be for good. And I felt it, the fleeting sadness of knowing the great things that had happened in my time here were over. Here I had conquered the odds and emerged victorious and confident. And now I would leave behind the friendships and relationships that I feared would fade into nothingness with distance and time. "Sure," you tell your friends, "we'll stay in touch, and I'll be back." But you know it will never be the same. And it never is.

I left Daviess that spring for Lancaster County. And when August came again, I set off in my sagging T-Bird. Stuffed so full there was barely room for the driver, the car lumbered down the highway. I turned to the south and headed out. My destination: Bob Jones University in Greenville, South Carolina.

Bob Jones University. The place that almost rivals the Amish when it comes to legends and myths. Even back then, I was told, "If you tell someone you went to BJU, get ready to duck or pucker. Because you'll either get slugged or get kissed." It hasn't been quite that bad, but there's something to the saying. Over the years, I've heard just about every rumor there is about how things really are on campus. And always, when I hear the stories, I just laugh and shake my head. "Where did you hear a thing like that? Are you sure it's true? Well, let me tell you how it was when I went there, back in 1991–93."

And people kind of draw back, astounded. "You attended there? But you seem so, well, nice. How could a guy like you have come from a place like that?"

Maybe because the "place like that" isn't quite the ignorant dump you think it is, I think. But I usually just bite my tongue.

"It's a racist school," some people have snarled contemptuously. "It's militaristic," my leftist friends have gasped in horror. But the most persistent myth I've run into is "Oh, yeah, that's the place where they have separate sidewalks for guys and girls." Countless people know that without the slightest doubt. Even when I tell them I was there and never saw such a thing, it's still true in their minds. It's all a bit strange. It's like facts don't matter.

I will always be proud to be a BJU grad, and I look back on those years with a lot of fond memories. A few negative things cropped up here and there, sure, but those will come at you in any setting. I walked into BJU mostly intimidated. I'd heard how tough it was academically. And how it had, like, a thousand rules of conduct. But still, I chose to go. Because at that moment, it seemed like the best choice. Or at least the choice I was most comfortable with.

And looking back, it was almost lackadaisical, how it all worked out that I ended up at Bob Jones. It could have been just about anywhere else. Notre Dame, even, if Dr. Pierpont had gotten his way. Somehow, though, a few figures I admired in my Plain Mennonite world steered me there. Sang the praises of the place. So I sent for an application during my second year at Vincennes. Filled it out and mailed it in. I was, of course, accepted. *Right on,* I thought. *This will be the place for me.*

The rule book they sent made me a little uneasy. Dress codes, infinite specific rules of conduct, restrictions on how long your hair may be, and on and on. I had just emerged from a world of infinite rules, there with the Amish. But I was comfortable in a structured setting, I think. However tough the rules, I could take it if I set my mind to it. That was what I figured. Besides, a few other things drew me there.

The first and primary thing: I had family in the area. My older sister Magdalena and my older brother Jesse and their families lived over close to Abbeville. And my youngest brother, Nathan, lived and worked in Seneca. All points within an hour's drive or so of Greenville. I'd hang out on weekends. And that strong pull of family settled it in my head. But there was still more.

I arrived at BJU a few days before my thirtieth birthday. Students have to live on campus until age twenty-five. After that, they can live off campus and work. Basically have a normal life. And that was what I planned on doing. And with my head swimming with vague, great dreams, I pulled into Greenville. Eagerly. I was here, whatever might come. And, of course, a few snags lunged up instantly. My planned lodging didn't work out, and the IHOP restaurant manager who had promised me a waiter job reneged when I walked in. Eventually, though, I found another waiter job at Swensen's Ice Cream Gazebo, and lodging in a little trailer park near the campus.

Some kindly, simple guy named Jim had a spare bedroom in his trailer. He'd prayed about it, he told me later, and decided he would rent it out. Everyone around BJU always seemed to be praying about every little thing. I guess that way, they could blame God if things didn't work out. Anyway, my simple friend Jim claimed he felt good about it. And I just happened to show up through a friend of a friend. Randomly. We had little in common, which I've found makes for the best roommates. In our daily interactions, we talked and got a glimpse of each other's world. But otherwise, no expectations.

It was late August, and it was hot. I timidly walked about the campus, trying to get my bearings. Lots of clean-cut people swarmed about. Students, teachers, administrators, and more students. Everyone seemed positive and upbeat. At least they smiled as if they were. I signed up for my classes and got ready for the first day.

It's a beautiful place, the university. Impeccably groomed grounds. Whatever was done there was done right. That attitude permeated the place. BJU is a Fundamentalist Baptist school where everything is done for the Lord. It's pretty much a self-sufficient campus, complete with a hospital, a large modern auditorium, the greatest collection of old religious art in the world (or one of them), its own security, complete with its own version of cop cars, dorms, and classrooms. And I realized on the first day that I wasn't in Vincennes anymore. Not in any sense, including the quality of the education. Not knocking Vincennes, here. Just saying, a private four-year university is going to be much tougher slogging.

During my second year at Vincennes, I took twenty-one hours of classes both semesters. And easily breezed right through. At BJU, I bravely signed up for eighteen hours the first semester. Surely I could handle that much. But before the first week ended, I did what I never thought I'd do. I dropped a class, reducing my load to fifteen hours. And even that seemed overwhelming. These people smiled and smiled. And then they piled on the workload and upped the expectations. They demanded the very best efforts from all their students. You won't sail through any classes at BJU. I can guarantee you that.

And I uneasily settled into my routine. This was a new place, an entirely new culture. Everyone looked and dressed the same, pretty much. Skirts and blouses for the women, suits and ties and wing tips or tasseled loafers for the guys, at least until noon. You had to dress up in the morning. This was a serious problem for me. I had never really learned to "dress up," so my wardrobe was quite limited. A half dozen shirts. Four or five dress pants. But mostly, I dreaded the mornings because I was different. And being "different" was a big part of the reason I could not abide with the Amish.

Back at Mount Olive Mennonite Church in Daviess, the women wore coverings. And the men wore those detestable straight-cut suit coats with no tie. When I entered BJU, I had never worn a tie. Never, in all my life. I came from a place where sermons were preached about how a tie can be only a symbol of pride. And to their credit, the BJU people made a rare exception in their rigid rules for Mennonites like me. I was allowed to wear the detestable straight-cut suit coat with no tie. Because my church had a rule. The people at Bob Jones knew all about rules.

But my detestable suit coat was so different and I was so painfully aware of that difference that it almost ruined my first semester. Everyone was staring at me. I could feel it wherever I went. In class. Walking about. And at chapel. As the weeks crept by, I actually nursed in my heart the vague hope that some mild misfortune would befall me, so I could get out of this place with some dignity. Something, anything, that's what I wished for. Maybe an accident, like a broken arm or leg. That would do it. I could leave and never look back. But no such misfortune ever showed up. There was nothing else to do but stay. So I slogged on, day after dreary, dreadful day.

In the meantime, though, I faithfully trudged to classes every day, too. Kind of found the rhythm of the place. Go to class, find your seat in the back. The professor takes roll call. And then we bow our heads to pray. The professor speaks to God for ten or twenty seconds. And then it was down to the business of learning.

I've thought about it since, now and then, all that praying going on. And it seemed to me after a month or so that these people weren't that different from the Amish, not when it came to praying. No, they didn't use a little black book. But their prayers were rote. How could they not be? I mean, how fresh can a prayer be, how heartfelt can it be when it's mandated? When it's just spouted out like clockwork? I might be way off here. I'm not saying the prayers weren't valid or that they weren't heard. But even way back then, fresh as I was from the Amish culture, I recognized the formula of the prayers on campus at Bob Jones.

And every weekday morning around ten thirty or so, the entire student body trudged off to chapel in the huge new modern auditorium. Forty-five minutes or so. That was how long it lasted. Attendance was mandatory, of course. You had your assigned seat, and ushers checked at every service to make sure you were there unless you had a valid excuse. I'm not knocking the practice. Not at all. I soon reached the point where I actually looked forward to chapel services, because the quality and depth of the preaching was so far beyond anything I had ever heard before.

And I heard all the guys who were anyone back in those days. Dr. Bob Jones Jr. was a grizzled, bent old man in his eighties, but he could sure punch out a good sermon. He roared like a lion and cooed like a dove. Hellfire and brim-stone. Come to Jesus. It was old-time southern preaching from a century ago, and I feel privileged to have heard it from him. And we heard Dr. Bob Jones III, too, a tall gaunt man with a harsh rasping voice. His sermons tended toward vitriolic diatribes against the evil Catholic Church and the occasional broadside against the "false teachings" of Billy Graham. These guys were exclusionary, oh yes, they were. Which I've never had a problem with, because that's what freedom of religion is. The freedom not only to worship as you see fit but also the freedom to exclude. Like the Amish exclude anyone who is not a part of their group.

And I heard, too, the sermons of various local preach-ers and the many preacher boys in training at BJU. It was quite an honor for them, I learned, to get asked to preach at chapel. And for the first time in my life, I grasped what it was to really dig into the Scriptures. Amish sermons are mostly extemporaneous, often rambling. The Mennonites I had joined were a little more prepared with their sermons, but still, they tended to bounce all over the place while preaching a lot of light fluffy stuff with neat little lessons wrapped up at the end. Not the BJU guys. They got up there behind the podium and belted out an entire half-hour sermon, not from one chapter. But from one verse, sometimes. And sometimes one phrase from one verse. I marveled at it all, the apologetics of Christian Fundamentalism. And I absorbed their words.

And while I thought their messages edged to the harsher side of Christianity, I didn't fuss unduly in my mind. I would take from this place what I could and apply it to my life. And besides, I wasn't quite sure where I stood on many peripheral issues. Hey, I would be there for two years. Then I'd move on, back to my little Mennonite world. That was my plan back then. Maybe I could even tell them about this marvelous in-depth preaching I had heard at BJU (that's a joke).

There was one aspect of their teachings that bugged me, though. And that was their eschatology. Their end-times teachings. BJU is (or was back then) stridently pre-tribulation rapture. Jesus is returning very soon, maybe even today or tonight. We'll all get raptured out to meet Him in midair, Dr. Bob III would thunder. Then the great tribulation will be unleashed upon the earth. Satan will take over the whole world. He'll take over this university, too, and use it for his evil purposes. But we'll be with God, up there, so it won't matter what Satan does down here.

But wait a minute, I thought, even back then. *If Jesus is coming back soon, maybe tonight, for sure by next week, next month, or maybe even as late as next year, why are we at this university? Why am I paying you for an education? Why are you demanding my best efforts in my classes? What sense does that make? Why plan for the future, why study for the future, why get a degree for the future, if it will all be for naught?* I couldn't quite grasp that line of thinking. And it still makes no sense to me.

And it's still one of the most shortsighted, destructive teachings in all of Christendom, that pre-tribulation-rapture stuff. My opinion. And it's certainly not exclusive to the BJU people. It's embraced by millions of Christians from many denominations, people who cling to the desperate hope that somehow they won't have to die. To all of them, I'll say this: Stop fretting about the end of the world or about Christ's return. <u>Get on with living your life with joy in this moment.</u> And instruct your children as if they will have a long life, too, and a productive future. Stop hoping not to die. I believe that every person alive today and those to come for many generations will one day die. And if I'm wrong, hey, I'll gladly concede my error in midair. "I was wrong." What I'm saying is, concern yourself with your own life and your heart before God. The "end of the world" will come for each of us when we pass from this earth.

By the time the first semester ended, I was just stepping into full stride. I came through with decent grades, mostly A's. And I changed my major from English education to straight English, against the advice of my professors. "What will you do with an English degree?" they asked. "I don't know and I don't care," I said. "I want to study real literature here. I want to absorb the great works of the past." They backed off then. And I walked forward into the classes my heart instinctively cried for. The classics: Shakespeare. Dante's *Inferno*. Milton. The major poets: Marvell. Pope. Keats. Shelley. And Emily Dickinson, one of my favorites. American literature: Mark Twain. William Cullen Bryant's "Thanatopsis." Faulkner, who ran with his coonhounds and hick country buddies at night and churned out his writings during the day. And on and on. I devoured it all. Guided by some of the greatest teachers I have ever known.

And after that first semester, my detestable straight-cut suit coat never bothered me again. I was who I was, and I was comfortable with that. If you had a problem with how

I dressed, that was your problem, not mine. And I made friends, both with my teachers and with many students.

At the beginning of my second year, I stumbled upon the greatest literary voice ever to emerge from the American landscape. Thomas Wolfe. I didn't meet him in the classroom. I just randomly picked up a ragged paperback copy of *You Can't Go Home Again* at a used bookstore. I took the book home and opened it. Began to read. And from the first page, I was hooked. Between classes and work, I devoured the book in the next week. I stumbled about, my head in a daze, barely conscious of the world outside those pages. His powerful, passionate, soaring prose spoke to me like none other ever had. Stirred something deep inside. Absorbing it all, I sensed the innate knowledge in my heart that one day I, too, would write my story. I would speak it to the world. I had no clue when or how. It was just a thing I knew.

There were many good things about BJU, not least its high appreciation for the arts. The university was saturated with performance art. Shakespeare plays of the highest quality, with faculty and students playing all the roles. Internationally acclaimed orchestras twice a year or so. Opera, performed by professionals. And classical music in all its forms. And we were required to attend. To which I thought, *What? Required to attend? You couldn't keep me away.* To me, it was a huge privilege. And I went, sometimes with a woman, always dressed in my straight-cut suit, and just drank it all in. Those moments remain among my most cherished memories of BJU.

And life in general bumped along. Every fall, when the students returned, the university held several nights of "revival" meetings in the big new auditorium. Good old down-home gospel preaching for the lost. And during those meetings, they fully expected people to stand, to recommit, to be saved if lost. Maybe even be re-saved. Dr. Bob Jr., the old man, officiated over both of the annual revivals I attended.

And he preached the gospel. Because Christ was proclaimed. But at the end, he unleashed some of the most manipulative methods I have ever encountered. Just to get people to stand. He was determined that all six thousand people in the auditorium would be standing before he closed out the final night. First, he called out for the lost. If you don't know Jesus, you can know Him tonight. Won't you stand? We have people standing by to lead you through those steps. And that was fine. But then it was on to other goals. Do you have sin in your life? Unconfessed sin? It's not too late. Tonight is the night. And a great many people stood. And then it was if you want to be a better witness for Christ, stand. Who can resist that? And so on and on, all the way out to where if you didn't stand, you were admitting that you were lost.

The first year, of course, I leaped to my feet at some point late. By the second year, though, I was in no frame of mind to be led by a nose chain like a common simpleton. I wouldn't do it just because everyone else did. I dug in, irritated. Whatever he said, I wasn't going to be manipulated. Not this time. I would not stand. And I didn't as the drama intensified. His final call. Unless you are not a Christian, stand. I sat there stubbornly. I could feel the eyes around me. No. I will not stand. I will not. Dr. Bob Jr. closed it out then with a prayer that encompassed every soul in whatever state. Including mine. And there I sat.

As we were dismissed, one guy behind me came up and tapped my shoulder. Smiled hesitantly. "Here's my phone number," he said, handing me a little torn slip of paper. "Call me if you want to talk."

"Nope," I replied. "I'm fine." And I walked out of there in my detestable straight-cut suit coat, the only Mennonite in the place. And one of the few deemed "lost." I also emerged with a new perspective on how things really are sometimes. And so my second year began.

A place like BJU could not function without toadies. Students who cozied up as aides to the big pooh-bahs, students who were "groomed" for leadership. Toadies were universally despised by the average students. And toadies were also indispensable to keeping the system running smoothly. Especially the system of demerits.

There were demerits for just about any imaginable offense. You could get a demerit for thinking wrong, I think. But mostly it was stuff like being late for class or not showing up for daily chapel service (we all had assigned seats, and ushers checked to make sure they were filled). There were also more serious but not unheard-of offenses like drinking, smoking, and touching someone of the opposite sex. You were never, never supposed to be alone with anyone of the opposite sex, in any room or place, anywhere. But probably the most detested of all demerits, at least for the guys, was the dreaded weekly (or biweekly, I can't remember) "hair check" when you walked into chapel for the morning service.

You never knew for sure which day would be hair-check day. Sometimes the word buzzed that it was such and such a morning. But you could always tell as you approached the entrance to the massive auditorium. Extra toadies with craning necks stood on each side. And as you walked by, you could feel their eyes scanning your hairline from the back, checking to make sure your hair wasn't a shade too long.

And one morning, during my fourth and final semester there, I got nailed. A tap on my shoulder. I turned in surprise. I'd never been bothered before. An ugly little toady stood there, in shabby suit and tie, frozen smile and all. "Your hair won't pass," he said. He handed me a ticket. Five demerits. I stood there, outraged and appalled. My hair was not too long. I didn't say anything to the toady, that wouldn't have gotten me anywhere. But I seethed silently. And that afternoon I stopped by the dean of students' office.

The dean, a lean, gravelly-voiced, humorless man whose name I don't remember, was back in his inner sanctum and unavailable, his toady told me. What could he do for me?

I presented my demerit ticket. "I got it this morning. Look." I turned around and pointed to my hairline. "It's not too long. It's not. I want to see the dean to get the ticket reversed."

The toady smiled patronizingly. "That's not possible. He can't be disturbed right now," he said. His name was Henry, if I recall right.

I stood there stubbornly. "Then I'll wait," I said. "I'm graduating this spring, and I have never gotten a single demerit. I don't want one now, not for a judgment call like this. I'll wait."

Henry was perturbed, not used to such blatant obtuseness. "Look, the ticket is what it is," he protested.

"Then I'll wait for the Dean," I said. And back and forth we went for a few minutes.

When he finally grasped that I was really not going anywhere, he suddenly reached out, took the vile little slip of paper, and tore it in half. "All right, then, there you go," he said resignedly. "I'll make sure it's struck from the records."

"You're the man," I said, shaking his hand. "Thanks very much." And I was out of there before the dean could appear and mess it all up again.

I never did get a single demerit. Not in my two years there. It's such a rare and shining achievement that Dr. Bob III sent me a personally signed letter of congratulation after I left. One day, I think, I will frame that letter. If I can dig it out from wherever.

In the summer of 1993, I graduated from Bob Jones University magna cum laude with a degree in English and a minor in history. A degree that was not even accredited. BJU refuses accreditation from any government entity. The administration rejects it out of hand. Leave us alone. We are doing our work as we see fit. We are training the next generation of our people. And that's a thing I respect and understand and admire. I value my time spent there. I would stack a BJU education against any university in this country when it comes to academic standards. And I will always defend its right to be just exactly what it is.

The world is a funny place sometimes. You step out and start off on a path, not quite sure if it's really the right one. But you strike out on the journey and push through to the end. And years later, you look back and realize that whether or not it was precisely the right path, it was one you would not change if you could.

That's me, looking back on my entire experience at Bob Jones University. I would not change a single moment in that stretch of the journey, not even if I could.

HOME FOR CHRISTMAS

IN THE FALL, we always stirred. Plotted. Prepared. Planned. Turned our faces again to the west and north and the distant land of home. Did whatever it took to make the long journey back for Christmas.

Those years in the early 1990s seem blurred now, as if they had all flowed together. Every year, my brother Nathan and I discussed it some throughout the summer, then got serious about mid-November. We didn't live close to each other, so plans had to be made. To get together and go home together.

By then I had graduated from Vincennes and had transferred to Bob Jones University in Greenville, South Carolina. Nathan lived an hour away, in the Seneca area. We existed on shoestring budgets. I was a student, and Nathan worked on a framing crew while he prepared for a one-year stint as a counselor at a boys' wilderness camp.

We were going home for Christmas. Home to our parents' two-hundred-acre farm in Bloomfield, Iowa, the place where only a few short years before, we had lived as Amish youth. Where we had grown into adulthood, where we'd run around. Where we had sown the seeds of that turbulent period of our lives and where we had eventually torn away, leaving in our wakes the trails of grief and pain, the dashed expectations of our parents and the broken dreams of others.

And we harbored in our hearts some few tattered remnants of regret and guilt.

We'd left independently, each on his own path and on his own terms. With little guidance, even less support, and no semblance of a safety net, we had pressed onward and outward. Walked away from the only family structure we had ever known. Driven by a vague, undefined hope, the desire for so much more, and always the promise of a brighter future, the distant gleam of a shining city in a tomorrow that never came.

Both of us were somewhat skittish, tense and raw. Un-healed. So little time had passed since we'd left. Back then, in our youth, a few years seemed like a long time. But it wasn't. And our internal turmoil could not be denied.

We had escaped the desolate land, the bleak deserts, the sparse, hard lifestyle, and we felt free. Why, then, return again into the dark boundaries of the land from which we'd fled? Because at Christmas, "home" was the only place we'd ever known. And despite the tension, the confrontations and admonitions we knew would come, we did not hesitate but prepared to set out on a journey back.

In a time before cell phones and email, we finalized the

details as the day came at us. My final test at Bob Jones was over by noon one day the following week. By midafternoon Nathan had arrived. Since we didn't trust either his little white pickup or my T-Bird to make the long trip, we pooled our meager resources (neither of us owned so much as a credit card) and rented a fire-engine-red Pontiac Grand Prix. We loaded our stuff and hit the road.

Through late afternoon and evening and long into the night, we drove, taking turns at the wheel, stopping only for gas and food and coffee. Few things dull the mind more than traveling all night in a car. Then into the sunrise, and on and on, the Pontiac pulsed along. North and west. By noon, we were getting close. We passed through the familiar northern-Missouri landscape. Crossed the border into Iowa and the first Amish farms on the southern end on Route 63.

We were back.

But first we turned east toward Bloomfield to buy some simple gifts. For Dad, a few boxes of Brach's chocolate-covered cherries. For Mom, a large red poinsettia. We cruised around the deserted town square. What only a few years ago had seemed like a glittering metropolis now sat squat and dark, a collection of ramshackle rusted stores huddled in a half-empty town.

Then we headed out of town, taking the highway west into the burg of West Grove and then right onto the gravel road that led to the farm. By two o'clock, we were pulling up to our parents' house.

It was all pretty much the same as it had been the last time. The old white bungalow with a few rickety buggies parked forlornly in front of the shop. We parked and got out and yawned and stretched and stretched. Then headed up the concrete walkway to the house, where Mom met us at the door. She smiled and smiled and chattered in welcome. Nathan handed her the poinsettia. She feigned surprise. Oh, for me! You shouldn't have. And we followed her into the warm, familiar kitchen, where her ever-present pot of coffee simmered on the humming stove. Sat at the table while she poured us each a cup.

She fluttered about and smiled and smiled. Her boys were home. And indeed we were.

After a few minutes, Dad, hearing the commotion, came clumping in from his tiny office attached to the north side of the house. He walked gingerly, limping on his gimpy knee. "Hello, boys," he said, peering over his wire-rimmed glasses at us.

And we stood respectfully and shook hands with him, and he spoke our names. We gave him his gift of chocolate cherries, and he sat down to visit a bit. How was the trip? Good, we said. Did you drive all night? Yes, we did. You must be tired. Yes, we are. And so on.

My father had an ironclad rule. No son who owned a car could live at his home. For the first few years after we left, his face darkened if we so much as drove a car onto his property and parked it for a short visit. But by the early nineties, we'd reached an uneasy, unspoken truce. He wouldn't fuss overmuch if we parked our car out front, as long as it was clearly understood that it would be only for a few days. Over Christmas, for instance. We honored the truce. And to his credit, so did he.

We settled in and sat around then, whiling away the late-afternoon hours, laughing and chatting with Mom as she bustled about, filling us in on all the latest local news while preparing supper. She hovered over the hot stove, stirring up a pot of her milk-based bean soup laced with herbs, because she knew it was our favorite. And she knew her kitchen was the only place in the whole wide world where we would ever find it.

Darkness fell, and the hissing mantel lanterns were lit, brightening the entire house. We sat down to eat, and it was a comfortable, pleasant thing. Just Dad and Mom and my brother and me. I know Dad was technically shunning me at the time, so I must have sat off to the side a bit, or we just ate cafeteria-style. Whatever it was, it was. Nobody made much fuss. After supper, we sat drowsily, nodding off on the couch. And as bedtime approached, Dad cleared his throat and announced it was time for evening prayer. We knelt and heard again the rich, mellow rhythm of my father's voice as he recited the five-minute High German evening prayer from memory.

At one point in these years—I don't remember exactly when—after the others had retired, I sat up with my father and we talked. Just he and I, man to man. He had many questions about my college classes and what I was learning. I was comfortable and open with him for the first time in my life. The hours passed, and the hissing lantern flickered low. At midnight, as the cold crept in, Dad got up and stirred the dying embers in the stove and restocked it with firewood. And with that, we finally went off to bed.

After that first time, we made it a tradition. The first

night of any future visit home, he and I would sit up late and talk. Those are among my most treasured memories of my father.

Nathan and I slept in the bedrooms that a few years ago had been our own. The smoky kerosene-oil lamp flickering dimly on the nightstand. The bed smothered with plump feather comforters Mom had carefully placed there. I snuggled in, the cold night air engulfed the room, and the high clear chimes of the old black wall clock struck once as I drifted off into fitful slumber.

The next morning I awoke early, startled by my surroundings. Dad called for us to come and eat the breakfast Mom had fixed. Eggs and bacon and toast and thick, rich gravy. Dad and Mom had usually already eaten, so there would be no awkwardness about shunning. Nathan and I sat at the table and groggily stuffed our faces with the food on which we had been raised.

After breakfast, Dad took up the Bible and read a passage of Scripture for devotions. Nathan and I glanced at each other. We might even have winked a bit. This was the ideal moment for the obligatory admonitions we knew would come at some point. We were trapped, a captive audience. It was Dad's time to deliver a mini-sermon about how we were living in the world and of the world. How we should even now change and return home and establish ourselves as upstanding members of the Amish Church. "Me and Mom believe that's the right thing for you to do." *Me and Mom*. Mom never had any voice in the matter. She was just included in the narrative. That's how he always wrapped it up.

Might as well get it out of the way, we figured, and get on with things.

And so he did. The same old song, exactly as we'd heard it many times before. Just a slightly different verse. Seems like it must have been a Bloomfield rule or something. If your worldly children come home to visit, make sure you lecture them. Don't let that chance slip by, or you will have sinned.

It would have been nice, just once, to go home and not be subjected to that particular refrain. But mostly, we learned to just let it pass and let it go.

After the obligatory lecture was over, Nathan and I thanked Mom for her delicious food and took off to tour our old haunts. Stopped to see our older brother Titus, who was calm and collected as always. Then to Chuck's Café in West Grove. Reconnected with the local farmers we used to hang with. Then around the settlement itself, stopping here and there to say hi to an old friend. And stopping by at our siblings' houses for coffee breaks and sweets.

Everywhere we went, the fire-engine-red Grand Prix was a source of great fascination. Someone must be doing well, people would comment slyly, to drive a car like that. We grunted vague replies and pretended the car was Nathan's. Didn't seem to cross anyone's mind that it might be a rental.

Bloomfield was expanding. Every year, it seemed new buildings had sprouted where only pasture grasses had waved before. Or some English farm had been snatched up by an Amish farmer. The character of the community changed. New names, new faces from people we had never seen before, people who had moved in from Jamesport, Missouri, and other troubled settlements.

The day slipped by and another night. And then Christmas dawned. We slept in, awoke late, and got up to Mom's fresh coffee. For the Scripture reading that morning, Dad read the Christmas story from Luke. No short sermons forthcoming this time. That little chore had already been done. Mom bustled about, covering hot dishes to take to the noon meal at my brother Joseph's house halfway out the lane. By eleven, a line of buggies trickled in. All the family gathered, as we always did on this day.

Nathan and I joined them. A large group. Our brothers and their wives, our sisters and their husbands. And all their children. The house soon echoed with our boisterous talk and great peals of laughter, common sounds at any Wagler gathering. A ragtag line of nephews hung in the shadows, rough and rugged boys, growing like weeds. They spoke shyly to their "English" uncles and discussed us among themselves. Soon enough, they, too, or a good percentage of them, would taste of the world outside the boundaries of their own.

A sumptuous feast was spread, and we gathered about. Heads bowed as my father prayed the blessing. And then we dug into the food.

After lunch, as everyone lounged around, dozing and drowsy, Nate and I made noises to depart. It was best to start back that day, to beat the heavy post-holiday traffic. Dad wished us safe travels. Mom gripped our hands and smiled and slipped us small gifts of stocking caps and gloves or similar practical things.

And then we left. It was time to go. We could feel it.

This was not our world. It would never be our world again. Sure, it was "home," but in cold, hard reality, we were strangers. We didn't fit, and we didn't belong.

And as we absorbed that truth, the deep stirring desire to return home for Christmas diminished in our hearts. Receded gradually, almost imperceptibly. Until it pretty much died, and we could find little reason to go back.

LAW SCHOOL

IT'S A THING of wonder and some amazement now, when I take the time to stop and think about it. Not that I do, much. One of the strangest little side trips of my life, in a long and distinguished line of strange little side trips. That's what going to law school was. I've often thought to myself, *What were you thinking? If you wanted to get educated about as far away from Amish roots as possible, law school would be the place.* And Dad? I think he was so astonished that he didn't have much energy left to protest. Oh, sure. He huffed and puffed around a bit. But he did that all through my college years, too. Maybe I had worn him down, or at least his power of resistance had been greatly diminished.

I mean, you think about it. The Amish and the law. The two mix about like oil and water. The Amish don't trust the state. They never have, and for good reasons. Our ancestors were hunted down like wild animals and killed by the authorities. Burned. Beheaded. Drowned. The Amish code of conduct includes a few simple rules that are passed on by word of mouth from hundreds of years of ancestral memories. Do not ever, ever trust the state, do not go to war, and never call on the law to protect you if you are wronged. The law. You obey it, as long as it does not get in the way of your duty to God. You try not to get entangled any more than you need to. You hang low, you walk quiet and humble. You never, never poke the beast. And here I was, walking into a jungle like that to learn the laws and the ways of worldly people.

That had to be a shock for Dad, right there. Or maybe not. I had already ventured out and conquered college. I think Dad was half-envious of that. By the time I got around to going to law school, he probably wasn't all that surprised. He might even have mentioned the matter with awkward pride to visitors when they came around. My son Ira is in law school. He was overheard saying that. Just never that I saw or heard.

The Amish don't shun lawyers entirely. You can't, in today's world. You have to use lawyers for transactional things, to survive. Things like buying and selling farms. Setting up a business. An attorney will write it all up. But the Amish do not sue. Well, I can't say never. There are always exceptions. One or two who will step out of line and go after their rights. That happens in any group, I guess. But I remember that when I was growing up, Dad didn't believe in calling the cops. Not for any reason. That was what he claimed. We never had much of a reason to, so Dad's resolve was never really tested that I saw. I don't know what he would have done, had an English person robbed him or invaded his home. I imagine he would have cooperated with the police. I don't know that. But anyhow. That's the background I came from. And now I was heading to law school to learn how to be a mean, wicked attorney. I think that was how a lot of my people saw it back then.

It was a long time ago, when it happened. A little bit of background on how it all came about. I graduated from Bob Jones in the summer of 1993. I wanted to take a year and work, to save up a little money for the next level. And to take a break for a bit. You get burned out with too much schooling. It's still a little foggy to me exactly how I got roped in. But I did. For one year I was a teacher at a private Mennonite high school in the next county north, which was Lebanon. I walked into that classroom the first morning dressed pretty dapper for a teacher in a Plain Mennonite school. I smiled at the students. There were probably thirty kids, total, in all four high school grades. I smiled first. Then I looked grim. "I'm a new guy," I told them. "I've never taught school before. But here I am. This is a new day. A new dawn. There will be order and there will be discipline."

The students smiled back. And a few of the ringleaders took it upon themselves to test me out those first few days. When that happened, I didn't smile. I looked mean and hard and grim. Mess with me, I signaled to the ringleaders, and you will pay. They weren't bad kids. Just lively and used to doing what they wanted to. I was a hard-core disciplinarian, but I was fair. And the days passed into weeks, which passed into months. And the school year flowed right by and passed, there at Lebanon Valley Christian School.

I wished my students well. And maybe it was just because they knew it was safe to say because I wasn't coming back, but a lot of them told me they wished I would come back and teach again. I was honored by those words.

After that year, I was done with my break. Ready to head on to new roads, more education. In the fall of 1994, I walked into the Dickinson School of Law in Carlisle, Pennsylvania, as a student for the first time. I was excited, of course. A little scared, too. I guess I was thinking a lot of things, not all of them practical. I knew I wanted to keep on getting my education. I was the first in my family to go to college. That broke every mold. And now I'd go for one more level, I figured. Either a master's degree of some sort, probably in English, or something like law. It would be cool to go to law school. About as far from my Amish roots as one could imagine. Those things were all factors. And I wondered, too, Could I really do it? I mean, there are a lot of legends out there about how tough law school is.

I remember that summer before I started. I had enrolled, you have to get that done way early. So I went through all those steps. Took the LSAT. I went and sat for that test without ever cracking a single book to prepare for it. These days, you can take courses to get ready for big tests like that. You probably could back then, too, in the early 1990s. I just wasn't all that tuned in. Plus, I'm sure I would have grumbled at the cost. My budget was a shoestring, as it was for years after that. Anyway, I just signed up and went and took the test and did OK. Not stellar. But respectable. That's how I scored. Respectable.

And I was excited, walking in as a student. Law school.

They made movies about how tough it was to go to law school. That old classic scene where the aged and learned professor looks disdainfully at his class for the first time never happened. The students are mostly guys in the classic scene. The professor addresses them with words to the effect of "Gentlemen. I want you to look to the right and to the left, at the two people beside you. When this semester ends, one of the three of you will have washed out." That didn't happen. The stodgy old professor couldn't have addressed us as "gentlemen," because a lot of the students in the Dickinson Law class of 1997 were women. Half the class, I'd say, or more. And a third of the students didn't flunk out, either. Had the studies been that hard, I doubt that so many of us would have enrolled. You can't have that, not when you're the oldest independent law school in the country. Which Dickinson was, back then. Not anymore, though. My class was the last one to graduate from an independent Dickinson.

I don't know. It was so long ago. Life in law school was intense, especially the first few months of the first semester. I remember you could have cut the tension with a knife. Small knots of students shuttled about, tense and nervous. The second- and third-year students looked at us frantic first-years, all bored. Get over yourselves. First-year law students (called 1Ls) took mostly core courses. The first semester, especially. Torts. Contracts. Property. Uniform Commercial Code. A few others that escape me at the moment. It didn't take me long to see this was a new level. Here, the students were motivated. They were here because they chose to be, not because their parents sent them. And they were here to graduate as high as they could in their class. It was a little shocking to me, to absorb and react to that level of competition.

In law school, I didn't work part-time waiting on tables. There was no time for that, I figured. I boarded in a dorm room for the first time in my life. The Curtilage, the place was called. It was what dorm rooms have always been, I guess. A place with a narrow little hard bed, a desk, a chair, and a closet. You had to otherwise furnish it yourself. At least the rooms were private. One student per room.

I settled in that first semester. Got to know a few people. Made some friends. By the second year, I had settled into the social schedule of the law school, too. Two things happened every week, like clockwork. Every Friday afternoon—well, late afternoon, after classes—there was a beer party at the Curtilage. Several kegs of quality beer. I never was much of a beer man, then or later, when the alcohol came calling. But I usually took a red Solo cup and filled it with the frothy brew and mingled and socialized. The second thing that happened like clockwork every week was we went to Blondie's Inn down on the main stretch. Not sure if the place is there anymore. Years ago, I heard some mumblings about a fire. Anyway, the place was packed, so you could barely turn around. A massive crowd of law students closed the place down every week.

The first year, I never went to Blondie's much, because I didn't drink much. That changed by year two, for whatever reason, and for better or worse. Before that, and through all my Amish years of Rumspringa and other frantic running, I never, ever had any issues with alcohol. Then, during my second year of law school, I discovered single-malt scotch. That stuff is an acquired taste, so I was putting on airs, probably, at first. Lawyers drink scotch. I was going to be a lawyer. Voilà. And by the time the second year wrapped up, I was drinking some sort of whiskey pretty much every night of the week. That long journey was just beginning. The hard road stretched before me.

I have many good memories of my three years at Dickinson Law. I got to know a lot of people and made some friends I'm still connected with today. The first semester, I got close to several women in one of my classes. We formed our own little study group, me and those three women. Kelly, Kimberly (or Kim), and Karen. Ira and the Special Ks, someone called us, and so we called ourselves that, too. Me and the Special Ks had many good times during those three rather intense years of studying at Dickinson.

Ever since leaving the Amish decades before, I had been vaguely conscious of the fact that there was a certain subset of people out there. The beautiful people. They'd always been around. I just wasn't always aware of them. They first nudged their way into my life (in a way that I noticed) at Bob Jones University, back in the early 1990s. I was too busy to pay them much mind, but I saw them. The GQ guys, always impeccably dressed. The guys who combed their hair swept off to the side, held in place by some high-shine hair grease. Pomade, I learned later it's called. They wore the latest cool shirts and khaki pants and shiny new leather belts and loafers. The women had it a bit harder, having to wear skirts and all. Still, they stood out, too. It took a while for the whole scene to work itself into my awareness. Don't get me wrong. The beautiful people were never rude, there at BJU. Just cooler than you could ever hope to be.

I remember, too, how Dr. Bob III, a gaunt giant of a man, ranted and raved against the beautiful people one day in his chapel sermon. They had all the wrong priorities, he roared from the pulpit. All their beautiful clothes and their cutting-edge styles would go down in flames and end up as dust and ashes. The Lord was not ever pleased with such things. I heard that sermon, dressed in my detestable plain-cut suit coat. I looked around and felt a little bad for the beautiful people. It took so much effort to look and dress like that. And now Dr. Bob was hollering at them. Oh well. I shrugged. It was a world I never knew or could even remotely imagine. I was a peasant, judging the elites of worldly society with disdain.

I walked on through life, far from the beautiful people. And it's not that I considered myself particularly ragged or uncouth. I was just a guy who had emerged from a plain and simple place. I was clean enough, I felt. I splashed my face with Skin Bracer or some sort of cologne every day before heading out to classes or, in summer, to work in the construction world. Around that time, a friend pulled me aside one day. She was the wife of a friend of mine, and she told me, "You're wearing too much cologne. It's too strong. Be more discreet." I was very embarrassed, but I thanked her and meant it. After that, I splashed on way less of whatever it was I was using.

Going forward, I never paid much attention to the beautiful people. I was too busy to be bothered by them. And I had my own issues in life. But there was one other place

I saw where those people proliferated. Law school. There, they were beautiful, and they were just a little bit better. Always impeccably polite, of course. And nice, too, and friendly. But it sank through my dense head in those three years. These people lived on a different planet than the one I came from. I would have little chance of ever associating with them, of ever really being accepted by them. Their women were off limits to me. Not that the realization of any of that was a big deal. But at this level, relationships mattered. Connections mattered. And the beautiful people looked out for each other. I was never really perturbed by it back then. In retrospect, well, that's how it was and how it went. I saw what I saw.

I entered my third and final year of law school. I wasn't intimidated by the law school schedule anymore by then. A bunch of us were older in the Dickinson Law graduating class of 1997. We'd been around and seen a few things. We weren't swayed easily from what we knew. "Make me," we said. In academia, there are always visions of utopia. Teachers and students discuss how this law or that law could improve our lives. We weren't taken with such talk, me and many of my older classmates. We knew better. Life is inherently unfair. And life gets messy. You can't make things better by decree. Someone, somewhere, is going to hold the power. Either the individual or the state. I always sided with individuals. Leave people alone to make their own decisions. Like the Amish. The more laws, the less freedom. I got a minor reputation for my "cranky" libertarian views.

Three years. A law degree is strange like that. Different.

They probably got tired of us, our professors. For sure by our third year. The final year. Didn't matter. We were who we were, and we all greatly anticipated our upcoming graduation. And it came down, in the spring of 1997. Decades ago, already. It was a clear and beautiful summer day. The ceremony was outdoors. I had some friends show up, even. After that first, lonely graduation from Vincennes, someone from my family always made it to the others. My brother Stephen had moved into the Lancaster area with his family a few years before. He came, along with his wife, Wilma. And my youngest brother, Nathan, flew up from his home in South Carolina. It was a big deal, I guess. Looking back, it still is. You graduate from Dickinson Law, you've done something.

I walked across the stage when my name was called late that beautiful, sunny morning. With a last name like Wagler, you're always going to be at the end of the line alphabetically in any graduation. The dean handed me my precious diploma, all nicely rolled up and tied with a ribbon. It's still all nicely rolled up and tied with that same ribbon, never framed. I guess my attitude reflects the world I grew up in. The Amish believe in doing, not in making a big fuss about what you've done. *I agree*

I studied for the Pennsylvania bar exam that summer. That whole thing is a racket, the bar exam. Dickinson prided itself back then—and still does, for all I know—on the fact that more than 90 percent of each graduating class passed the bar on the first try. I think it was 90 percent. It was high. My class did not disappoint. We kept the tradition going. I passed, too. I moved to Lancaster City, to a little apartment in a big complex on East Walnut Street. Up on the third floor, at the very top. I'd always had a hankering to be a city dweller like that. I walked every morning to the law offices of Clymer and Musser, on the first block of North Lime. I lasted four years as a practicing attorney. It was the only period in my life that I wore a suit and tie to work every day.

Law school was the closest thing to an aberration in all the decisions I made after leaving the Amish. I've never been able to articulate a really good reason why I went. It just seemed like a good idea at the time. Not sure why. Oh, there's a new door. Let's peek behind it. Law school. Why not? That's how lackadaisical it was, the whole journey. Go. Walk through it. See what happens. So I did.

ELLEN

CHRISTMAS DAY, 1998. I can't remember if it was cold. The skies were overcast. As was the norm on a holiday like that, I stopped at my brother Stephen's house for the noon meal. The Christmas feast. And we were just hanging around that afternoon. At some point, she arrived and walked in. Ellen. I had heard the name. She was a cousin to Stephen's wife, Wilma. From Missouri. She was a Yutzy, like Wilma was. Their fathers were brothers. And I heard her voice before I got up from the couch to meet her.

She was beautiful. That much was established in my mind in about two seconds. Medium tall at five feet four. And her smile dazzled me. We hit it off, right there, right then. Introductions were made. Ellen, this is Ira. Ira, this is Ellen. I offered my hand and smiled. And in minutes, we were laughing and chattering as if we had known each other for a long time. She hung out in the kitchen with the women then. And I sat with the guys there in the living room, by the nice crackling fireplace. By midafternoon, I made noises to leave. Still, I watched for my chance. And when she stood alone off to the side for a moment, I swooped in.

It was Christmas Day. New Year's Eve was coming right up. I had nothing planned. I mean, it wasn't like the lovely women were knocking down my door or anything. So, out there in the kitchen, standing by ourselves, I asked her, "Are you doing anything next Thursday night? New Year's Eve?"

She smiled at me. And she didn't hesitate. No, she didn't have much going on. "Would you like to go out?" I asked. And she smiled at me again. A big, warm smile. Sure. She'd love to go. I smiled back. I got her number and promised to call in a few days. And then I left for my dumpy little trailer home over in the Welsh Mountains of Lancaster County. My head was spinning.

I was pretty set in my ways back then. I guess I still am. I was in my late thirties. I had battled alone for so long, I just got tired of looking for someone who would walk with me. I drank lots of scotch whiskey to dull the pain of all I had seen and lived in the past. And all I had lost. So I wasn't really looking for Ellen when we met. It was a total aberration for me to ask her out like that.

I called a few days later, after the weekend, one evening. It had always been a freaky thing for me to call a woman, even though I had promised Ellen that I would. And she had welcomed that. Still. What if she regretted our little agreement to go out? What if she didn't want to talk to me all that much? I'm a little shy around women I like. Always have been. And if I get even the slightest inkling that the woman I'm talking to would rather not speak to me, well, I don't hang around long to analyze things. I don't beg or plead or stumble about with my hands in my pockets. Ah, shucks. You don't want to talk? I don't take the time to ask. I'm just gone, without a lot of noise, without much fuss or hassle. Still. I had promised Ellen that I would call. So that night, I took a deep breath. And I dialed her number. This was in 1998. My phone was a landline. That's startling. I called her on a landline, and she answered on the first ring.

It had been a few days since we'd met, but her voice was just the same. That lilting laugh. Yes, she had been expecting my call. And yes, she was eager to go out, still, on New Year's Eve. I relaxed. And we chatted. I told her, "I'll pick you up this Thursday at six thirty." And she told me where she lived. A few miles away, along Route 340, in a basement apartment with a friend. "I'll be there," I told her.

"I'm looking forward to it. See you then." And she laughed her lilting laugh. My head was spinning again as we hung up.

I don't know. What all do you include in one more story about a man meeting a woman and taking her out? It's a universal thing, and this is only the ten millionth time such a story has been told. Still. I guess the first date should take up a bit of space, some description. After that, it'll just be chunks and pieces. Too much detail is too much detail. The big day arrived, then evening came. I was driving a little white four-door Dodge Spirit, a fairly late model for me. 1990, I think it was. Compared to the ugly tan T-Bird, the white Spirit made me feel like a bold knight in gleaming armor, astride a gallant steed. And on my gallant steed, then, I rode to the lovely maiden's castle to get her out of there for the evening.

I won't pretend to remember what either of us wore that night. I could describe just about any spiffy outfit, and it would be completely credible. But I won't, because I don't remember. I was cleaned up pretty good in those days, at least for me. I wasn't overweight, not by much if any. And I was working as an attorney. I had to dress professionally for that. I had nice shirts and stuff. What Ellen wore, well, it was a dress of some kind. She looked stunning. And the one thing my eyes kept drifting to as the night went on was her beautiful chestnut hair. It was cut. There was no shred of a head covering. I knew where she had come from, and what a Plain place that was. As Plain as the Amish world I had come from, just in different ways. And I knew. To pull it off as comfortably and naturally as Ellen did that night, not to have any kind of head covering, well, that took a person with a lot of strength. You don't get to a place like that without fighting hard for it. So I not only admired Ellen's beauty on that first date. I respected it.

The Quality Inn and Suites over on Oregon Pike. That was where I took her. The place is gone now. Long since demolished. It had a pub and restaurant, and there was a New Year's Eve party. You had to have reservations to get in. It was one of the few venues that had anything open when I called a week before, after asking Ellen out. There were very few spaces left anywhere to book. So I was probably scraping the bottom of the barrel, going there. I thought nothing of it. I was just happy to have somewhere to take this beautiful woman.

The dining room was pretty much packed and hopping. We were seated at a nice little table for two, out in the middle of everything. I remember almost nothing of the food and just a few shreds of our conversation. And we danced. That I remember vividly. Slow tunes and fast. And as midnight approached, we danced to Prince's classic "1999." We whooped and shook our noisemakers as the new year swept in. 1999. It would be an interesting year. There would be good things.

It was bitterly, bitterly cold that night. That I remember, too. I had Ellen home by one thirty a.m. or so. We held each other and hugged good night. There was no question in my mind. I don't think there was any in hers, either. We definitely were going to be seeing a little bit of each other in the near future and beyond. You don't know after one date. But you know you'd like to know.

My little white Dodge steed crunched home through the snowy roads. I parked and walked through the bitter cold and ducked into the lovely warmth of my dumpy little trailer house. My dreams would be sweet that night.

And that was my first date with Ellen.

She came from a hard place, like I did. The Plain Mennonites. Similar to the Amish world I had emerged from. But tougher to break free from, if such a thing is possible. I didn't know that then. I learned it later, simply from getting to know Ellen and seeing how hard she tried to reach back into that world for some closure and acceptance and love that her father would never give. And I could see the hard place she came from because of choices she made years later, after we were married.

It certainly attracted us to each other, that we came from similar places. Her parents, Adin and Fanny Yutzy, had been raised Old Order Amish. Adin was a brother to the Yutzy men who had settled in Bloomfield. So Ellen was a first cousin to the five Yutzys who had married my siblings. Two of my brothers, Stephen and Titus, had married into the extended Yutzy family. As well as three of my sisters: Naomi, Rachel, and Rhoda. All of them had married Ellen's cousins. The blood mingled well, it seemed like. Yutzys and Waglers. And that was fine by me. As far as I was concerned, it could mingle one more time. And show the world that it works when you mix two wild bloods such as ours were.

I don't know what to say about our courtship, really. It was the same as thousands of other courtships, I suppose. The same but different. Because it was us. We got along well. We really did. And it didn't take but a month or so for me to tell her that I loved her. She knew it. She could tell. Still, to hear me say it kind of threw her for a loop. That's how women are, I guess. Or that was how Ellen was, at least. It didn't take her long to come back and tell me she loved me, too. Spring flowed into summer, and in August, I think, I was ready to pop the question.

And that night, I do remember. I made reservations at the Hotel Hershey in Hershey, Pennsylvania. It's about as high class a restaurant as you're going to get to in this area. It's very formal. And expensive. I remember the suit I wore, and I remember the color of Ellen's dress. Burgundy. And how beautiful she looked. She glowed. After a very nice formal dinner with wine and all the good vibes you could ask for, we went for a stroll out in the garden.

I was nervous. Of course I was. I knew she was half expecting to be asked, because we had talked about it. And we had even looked at rings in the mall a few months before. Still. Near as I can tell, a man is pretty much perpetually petrified when he's dating a woman. Especially when it comes time to ask her to marry him. He feels unsteady. Unsure. He weighs it all out in his head. The scales have to tip way over to one side before he'll ever convince himself that there's actually a better chance than not that she'll say yes. Then he lumbers about, all mysterious, to make it happen, and she acts gracious and does her best to look surprised and pleased. That's how all that works.

We strolled about, hand in hand. Dusk was settling in, and the pole lamps were lit. There weren't a lot of people around. And I waited until we were off on a side path, alone. And I tightened my arm around her. Whispered her name. "Ellen."

"Yes?" She stood, looking up intently into my face, into my eyes.

"Will you marry me?" I asked as I was getting down on one knee. You can plan all you want. In the actual moment, you stutter and stumble like a flustered schoolchild. At least, I did.

She smiled down at me. And she opened her arms wide. "Yes, Ira," she said. "Yes, yes, yes."

Relief washed through me in waves. Wow. How about that? She said yes.

We held each other, there in the lamplight. I murmured things, like you do when you're in love and just asked your woman to marry you. Ellen huddled close in my arms. We looked around then. She had a little camera with her. And we asked a guy who was strolling by, "Would you take our picture? We just got engaged." The guy of course claimed to be delighted to oblige. We posed in each other's arms. I haven't seen that picture in a long, long time. It's in a box somewhere in the garage. But I can still see it in my mind, as vivid as it actually was. Two smiling, beautiful people, looking eager and excited and happy. And ready to walk a new road together.

The fresh scent of sweet clover and the flowers in the garden drifted in the gentle evening breeze. And the banquet of life with all its rich and ample fare was spread before us like a feast. We were alone, lord and lady of vast domains, king and queen of all our eyes could see.

And midnight seemed far away, and we knew that we would be forever young.

WEDDING

WE GOT MARRIED on August 4, 2000. That's a pretty simple anchor date for me to remember as I get older and things that once were important aren't anymore. It was an exciting time in both our lives. Neither of us could ever have imagined how short a time this world we were in would last. We were young and free. Ellen beamed on my arm. I stood proud and tall beside her. Nothing would ever shake this world from what it was. Except death, of course. After we got old.

There was no doubt in my mind that Ellen and I were going to be together for as long as we both lived. I don't have any clue how English couples feel when they get married, the ones born English, I mean. Ellen and I both came from worlds where divorce was not an option, although it should have been. Well, maybe that's a little strong. Still. It's a fallen world, and every system gets abused. Divorce gets abused. So does not having the option of divorce. In any world where divorce is strictly forbidden, the women usually get suppressed pretty severely. A lot of Plain women (and English women in hard religious settings) out there just shut down emotionally. They have to, to survive. Not all of them, by any stretch. But a lot. There is simply no denying that.

August 4, 2000. A small crowd of guests gathered at a beautiful little wedding chapel in Gatlinburg, Tennessee. Quaint, cute, rustic, and almost impossibly small, the chapel sat nestled in the remote and wooded hills a few miles outside of town.

We had decided this would be the simplest way to get married. Leave town, tell our friends and family, and let come who may. Rent a chapel, rent the preacher. No fuss, no hassle, no six months of all the strain and stress and planning almost universally associated with weddings.

And it made sense to do that. We were both independent. Had lived on our own. I was a bit older, at thirty-eight. She was just shy of twenty-five. We were both transplants in the area where we lived. People would have to travel anyway to get there. Besides, neither of our sets of parents would attend our wedding, because it was too modern, too English. We didn't really think about it that much. It's just how it was. And that made the decision easier. Get out of town. Get it done. Then return.

And so the plans were made. And the date set. Friday, August 4, 2000. Twenty days before my thirty-ninth birthday. She located the chapel and made the calls. Planned the details. I shuffled about and tried to stay out of the way, emerging when needed, clutching my credit card to make the reservations I was told to make.

The date approached. Our excitement grew. Especially hers. I was more even-keeled, stoic. I had been comfortable on my own. I'd always figured I wouldn't marry until I met that one exceptional woman. If she never came, I wouldn't worry about it. I was pretty happy as I was.

We packed her car and headed out the day before the wedding. Drove south. After a full day's drive, we arrived in Tennessee, at the house rented by my brother and nephews for the occasion. A great party ensued, with much celebration.

The wedding day dawned. Beautiful, clear, cloudless. We rushed about in final preparation. Drove to the courthouse and picked up our marriage license. Went back to the house. Then to the chapel. The service would be at four that afternoon.

We met the pastor, a slight elderly man with a shock of gray hair, dressed in a long black robe. He carefully wrote down our names, and we chose the vows we would use. She then disappeared into her dressing room with her bridesmaids. I would not see her again until she walked the aisle toward me.

The groom retired to his dressing room. That was me, on the only day in my life that I ever was a groom. I donned a new black suit. New shoes. New shirt. And a new tie, trimmed in black and gold and burgundy. I swore I would never wear the tie again after the wedding but would always keep it as a memento of that day.

Guests arrived and wandered into the little chapel and seated themselves. About eighty in all. My siblings. Her siblings. A few friends. But not our parents. Not hers or mine. They refused to attend such a worldly affair. We'd never expected them to come. But they also refused to wish us well or bless the union. Well, it was both the fathers who were hard core. Our mothers simply loved us and always, always accepted us as much as they could get away with. Still, the fact remained that our parents would not attend or wish us well. That was pretty much like they released the equivalent of a curse instead, I've always thought. It just was. Our fragile bonds of marriage would have been stretched tight enough without all that extra pressure.

And then it was time. The elderly pastor led the groom and his attendants into the chapel through the little door in the rear. The pastor stood behind the podium. I stood to his left, the groomsmen spread to either side.

The music started. The little nieces walked up first, carrying baskets. Spreading silk flower petals along the aisle. Then came the bridesmaids, one by one.

The wedding march. All rose and turned, their eyes glued to the door. And she entered, a vision in white, a wisp of veiling obscuring her lovely face. Her older brother by her side, she walked up slowly and stood before the pastor.

"Who gives this woman to be married?" the good pastor intoned dramatically.

"Her family and I do," her brother answered almost inaudibly.

She stepped up onto the little platform and faced me. We held each other's hands. Looked into each other's eyes.

The pastor had performed a thousand such little ceremonies for people he'd never seen before or since. With practiced ease, he opened with a prayer, then read a short passage from the love chapter: 1 Corinthians 13. His calm voice rumbled through the tiny chapel. He then turned his attention to the excited, eager couple before him.

He addressed the bride. "Love your husband. Meet him at the end of each day with a smile. Comfort and encourage him as a man. The man. Your man. Be true to each other."

And then the groom. "Honor and love your wife. Look to her as you did during your courtship days. Let not sorrow cloud her brow or her eyes be dimmed with tears."

And then we exchanged vows. Slipped the rings onto each other's hands. By the power vested in him by the state of Tennessee, and before God, the pastor pronounced us husband and wife. Together we lit the large unity candle as Michael W. Smith sang her favorite song. And no, I don't remember what the song was.

The pastor then presented us to the assembled guests as husband and wife. And we walked out hand in hand as Aaron Tippin belted out one of my all-time favorite country songs, the words I chose to have engraved on the inside of my wedding band: "For you, I will." We stood at the entry of the little chapel and received accolades and congratulations from all our friends. The entire service had lasted nineteen minutes.

After the reception, during which everyone was amply fed, a group of our friends escorted us to a nearby nightclub for champagne and dancing. In the glitz of the night-club lights, we laughed and celebrated with uninhibited exuberance.

As the night hours slipped away, we held each other

close and slow-danced across the gleaming hardwood floor in the soft strobing lights. Our futures, our entire lives, lay before us. Together from this day.

We knew we would grow old together. That God's gentle hand would reach down and touch us and bless our lives with children. That we would live to see our children grow. That our sons would be as plants grown up in their youth and walk the land, tall and strong and confident. That our daughters would be as cornerstones and bring us great joy and honor.

That we would live lives rich and full of years. Until that inevitable hour when death called one of us away. And separated us.

This we knew in our hearts. As we danced the hours away on that enchanted, magical night.

STONE ANGEL

I REMEMBER THE breath and feel of that Saturday after-noon decades ago. Cool and cloudy, pretty much a normal March day. I remember it as a special day, unlike any I had seen before or have seen since. Because Ellen and I were going to check out a house someone had offered to us for sale. We wanted to see if it would be suitable for our first home.

We didn't have a lot back in those days. Not even the credit scores needed for a standard home loan. And this was back when credit was easy, compared to now. The thing was, August was coming right up, real soon. And the wedding date. We needed a place, a home to live in. I mentioned as much to one of my Amish customers one day, and he told me he had a house he'd sell us. It would be just what we needed, he thought. Not only that, he'd finance it for us, too. We were eager to see it. It would have to be pretty rough not to suit us, we figured. And that March afternoon we picked up the Amish man and took him over to check it out.

It was a nondescript house, really, right along the main drag on Route 23. Just a big, square, hip-roofed, two-story building on a small slanted lot. With a big old block garage off to the north side. But we were excited. And we walked through the place eagerly. It was pretty basic: four rooms and a stairwell leading down to a dank basement. And a small enclosed porch on the north side, with a very tiny bathroom with a shower stall on one end. The kitchen was fine just like it was, Ellen thought. And sure, the house was old and a little battered here and there, but we could see a home in it. Just tear out and replace some ugly old shag carpet, and it would be all we could ever dream of. We told the man we'd take it.

It was big and solidly built of bricks, the kind of house you see all around the area here. With a great many very large dull windows in every wall. "Good grief," I grumbled. "Why so many windows? Didn't they have electricity back then?" And these were old-style wood-framed windows, too, from all the way back to when the house was built in the late 1920s. Windows that would have to be replaced before too long. But you don't think about things like that, not when you're reaching out to grasp something you've never done before. We were young and eager, as any engaged couple would be. And we were impressed with the house. The upstairs was a rental unit, which would provide income to help pay the mortgage. That left the downstairs for us. It was functional, and that's about all it was. But we didn't need fancy. All we wanted was a home to call our own.

The price was good in the free market, the terms were

good as well. And within a few days, we signed an agreement of sale for the place. After the wedding, we'd transfer
it to joint ownership, as husband and wife. I handed the
man a check for $5,000, money that Ellen had carefully
scrimped for and saved. There was nothing even close to
that much money in my account. I had wandered pretty
much all my life. And believe me, from what I've seen, that
old saying is right on. A rolling stone does not gather any
moss. I can tell you that firsthand.

The closing date arrived, and we settled. The man signed
over the deed, and we signed the mortgage. And I took
it to the county courthouse, where such things are filed
and recorded. That's where the real estate records reflect
countless tales of dreams born and later shattered. As our
own record would show soon enough. And one Saturday
shortly after that, a few of my redneck buddies helped me
move in. And I lived here by myself. Ellen was over all the
time, of course, and we scraped together some furnishings
for the house, for when we would live in it together. A new
pale-green couch from a discount warehouse. An old table
and some chairs, scrapped from an auction somewhere.
Just your odd mixture of stuff to live with, stuff that makes
a home.

After the wedding, she moved in. Here we were, set up
in our own little home. And the neighbors hovered with
watchful eyes. We greeted them, got to know them a bit.
And they told us this old house had a pretty bad reputation
over a lot of years. Tenants drifted in and out, came and
went. And things got rowdy pretty often. Lots of yelling
and cursing and fighting going on. It was not unusual, the

neighbors claimed, to see cop cars at the place with lights flashing just about any time of the night. We just listened and smiled. Calmingly, I think. That kind of rowdiness was over in this house, we felt. No way anything like that will ever happen while we live here. And the neighbors seemed pleased and welcomed us.

The house was old and in disrepair. It had once stood grand and proud. But now, not so much. A lot of the mortar was missing in the brick joints. Long strips and little pocked places here and there. There was plenty of empty space between the bricks in the walls of the house. And all those windows were just flat-out worn out. A few were stuck, you couldn't even open them properly. And they were all old and leaky.

But it was soon visible to anyone who knew the place before. This time it was different. Not because of me, because I was pretty comfortable with the way things were outside. I'm a guy. Hey, if the place is half cleaned up, I'm cool with it. Just as it is. I'm not in competition with anyone to have the nicest place. I don't understand that mind-set.

Being that laid back is generally not acceptable to a woman, though. And Ellen had a few ideas about how we could improve the place, make it look better. The unkempt row of raggedy shrubs on the west side of the front porch, those had to go. "I want to plant flowers there," she said. Yes, dear. I borrowed a skid loader, and a friend helped me rip out the shrubs one Saturday morning. And then the flowers needed planting.

And over here, more beds to till and mulch. It all had to

be mulched. I never was aggressive about such things, but I did what I was told. And after the flowers came a garden. A little sliver of land, right on the west side of the garage. Probably ten by twenty feet, if that. I rented a little Honda tiller and broke and tilled the soil. And she planted her seeds. And soon the earth blossomed and brought forth its bounty. Tomatoes, lettuce, and all manner of other stuff. By the work of your hands and the sweat of your brow shall you eat. And we worked and ate the fruits of our labor. Those days were good. And the memories of them are good.

And we lived here, in this old house of formerly unsavory repute, for close to seven years together. Good years, some of them, and turbulent years, too, some of them, especially toward the end. Let's just say that two deeply hurting and flawed people could not see past each other's wounds and flaws. And things just went the way they did.

And yeah. I look back sometimes and wonder, When did it start? It's hard to pinpoint the spot where I would have realized our marriage was in trouble. A thing like that starts out gradually, most times, I'd say. The first few years went as first years do for newlyweds. We both worked. I dressed in suit and tie every day and went to my attorney's office. She worked as a licensed practical nurse while going to college part-time to earn her registered nurse's degree. A real nurse. Ellen was a natural, beloved by everyone she cared for.

We wanted children. Ellen would have made an excellent and natural mother. We tried to make it happen. And somehow, Ellen could not get pregnant. No baby. We grieved that. Well, she did more than I, probably. Still. I would have welcomed fatherhood, had that reality come knocking. I would have walked into it. I don't know. I've always thought I'd be a decent father. Probably a little more laid back, just because my own father tended to be uptight. No way I can tell how it would have been, though. Because it wasn't.

I don't know what else to tell about the seven years that passed. Somewhere in the middle, there was a little hiccup. My first realization that we had serious marriage issues. We separated for about six months. Ellen moved in with her older sister Arlene, who lived an hour west of our home. And we got back together on the first day of spring that year, the year of our rebuilding. We had come through some hard things. We had battled back. Now our eyes were bright with hope for the future.

It didn't last. I guess there was no way it could have. There were too many wounds in both our pasts, I think. A few years later, everything blew up again. For good, this time. Yeah, there are a lot of things that could be said about how it all went. Some bad choices were definitely made. Bad decisions. And there was a lot of pain and betrayal, too. I wandered in darkness and in rage for a while. And today, well, today, it's a little strange. I don't have a lot of details to tell. Still. From here, from where I am, still in this old house, I will say a few words about the aftermath.

I'm divorced. That fact alone makes my writings go down hard in a lot of places. Who can speak truth from a place like that? It's simple enough, such reasoning. It's a lockstep thing, that reaction. I'm divorced. The first in my family to reach that wretched milestone. Among the first in a long broad lineage of purest Amish blood. How can you possibly get to that point without hearing the echoes from all those voices from way back? That's how they told you it would go. And they may have been right. If you walk away from the safeguards you were taught, bad things will happen. And there's a whole lot of judgment coming at you from certain quarters when you do and it does. And a whole lot of Scripture spouted about how it all is sin. But not a lot of talking, eye to eye. Not a lot of listening, either.

And I concede. It's true. I walked away from a lot of the stuff I was told and taught. And yeah, things blew up on me, big time, here and there. But that doesn't mean bondage is superior to freedom. It's not. And it never was. Rattle those chains of the law all you want, and tell me how sweet it is to be imprisoned and safe. We all choose how we will live. And I choose to walk free. I will face the battles life throws at me. I will take some pretty heavy hits from those battles now and then. That's how life is when you really live it. I will show you the scars from those hits, those wounds, tell about them. I will walk on.

I'm not quite sure how it all happened, the thought process that brought a stone angel to our house. A little stamped concrete statue, mass-produced in China or some such place where labor is cheap. It's not like any stone statue could have much meaning to me. Except maybe this one. Maybe this stone angel meant more than I thought.

And it's strange, when I look back at it now, how it went with me and Ellen. Strange how we functioned in those final months before our parting, that heavy season of silent, almost unfathomable sorrow. We both knew what was coming. And it was a hard thing to face and walk through every day. But still, we got along. It's not like you can ignore each other when you see each other every day. When you live together in the same house. Things were tense and very sad, but you had to keep walking. And we did. Just kept living. And even laughing some. And one Saturday afternoon in December, we decided to go to Park City Center mall to do some shopping. It was my idea to go. And she may have needed a few things, maybe some Christmas gifts, and probably some things to take with her when she left. That date was looming, coming right up in March. "Mind if I go with?" she asked.

"Of course not. Come on. We'll go in my truck," I said. And off we went together to the mall.

We wandered about, mostly window-shopping, chatting amiably. And we drifted in and out of stores. I forget the name of the particular store where the angel was. It's not there anymore, hasn't been for years. A place where they had all kinds of odd and fascinating stuff. And I saw it standing there on display. A stone angel, about three feet high. Looking into the distance, wings folded, tiny hands clasped in prayer. I stood there, just engrossed. And it stirred in me shades of Thomas Wolfe, my hero. His famous first novel and the stone angel in his father's shop. Even his descriptive words applied, I thought: "Its stupid white face wore a smile of soft stone idiocy."

And I pointed and walked up to it. "Look at this angel," I told Ellen. "Isn't it beautiful? I think I want it."

She was more than agreeable. "If you want it, buy it," she told me. I forget the exact price. A hundred and thirty bucks sticks in my mind. Not the kind of money you just throw out there for nothing.

"Let me think about it," I said. And we walked around the mall some more for a while, dodging downstairs to the food court to grab something to eat. And it kept pulling me back, that store. "I'm going to go back and buy it," I told her. We walked back. And I bought my first ever angel with my Discover card. I proudly carried it out to my truck.

And I brought my stone angel home. "Right there, on the north edge of your garden, under the shrub tree, that's where I'll set it up," I told Ellen. And that's what I did. Set up the statue under the branches of that tree, on a little concrete slab. And it fit, the setting of it all, I thought. We were beyond help, we both knew that. But now an angel was standing there, looking at our home. Lifting its tiny stone hands in prayer.

The Lord knew and I knew. The broken road before me stretched into the wilderness, as far out as the eye could see.

MARCH IS THE CRUELEST MONTH

WE WERE IN trouble and we knew it. During the summer of 2006 we existed together, but that was all. And our marriage would soon be over as well. We spoke through the vast distance that separated us, our voices echoing in the darkness that was closing in from all around. We attended church together. Smiled in public. Even laughed together. Genuinely. People thought, *What a nice, well-adjusted couple. They so complement each other.* But the perception was false and hollow. And we knew it was not true.

We had separated once before, for six months. A few years before. We both had worked on what it took to get back together. Attended counseling sessions. Talked. We had reunited on the first day of spring, March 20. And everything went OK for a while. But something under the surface always rankled, something not right. She was unfulfilled. I did not trust her. Mired in the issues that had separated us, we soon drifted apart again. The shaky foundations we had built together deteriorated. Over time, into nothing.

That year, the summer drifted by, week by week. We talked now and then. Seriously, about our future and whether it would be with each other. We attended a relative's wedding out of state in June. Hung out with my family.

She had always wanted to see Valley Forge, so one Saturday morning in late August, we packed a picnic basket and drove there. Parked and got out. Walked the little paved path that traverses the perimeters of the camp and battlefield. Beautiful day. Windy, though. And unseasonably cool. Clouds obscured the sun for minutes at a time. We walked along, chatting amiably.

At the midpoint, we found a stone bench. And sat and talked. She told me she was leaving. I already knew. We had discussed it before. I didn't want her to go but didn't know what to say. I knew I couldn't convince her. She wanted actions, not words. I knew she was unfulfilled. Felt unpursued. She expressed her frustrations that day. She spoke clearly. Not in anger, but honestly, with feeling.

Gloom descended on me. I heard her speak, but her words might as well have been spoken in another language. "I will never be able to be what you want," I said. "The kind of man you want does not exist. Or marriage, either."

"You won't if that's how you feel," she said. "You won't even try."

I could live without her. I had seen and experienced hard things before. Brutal, life-altering things. Years ago, in another lifetime. Before I'd ever met her. Walked away when I thought it would kill me. It had taught me that when all else was stripped away, in silence or after all the words that could be spoken had been said, each person ultimately stood alone. And walked alone. There was no one I couldn't live without. No one. I had learned the lesson well. I would survive.

I looked at her, then away. At the people strolling past. I fleetingly wondered what problems they were facing. If any of them could relate to me and all that was going on. I turned back to her. "I have a lot of faults, I know," I said simply. "The way you say. But I'm a good man. And you know I'm a good man."

A white cotton-candy cloud swept across the sun. The air chilled instantly. We got up and walked on into the wind.

The weeks passed. Things were going on. And had been for most of the year. Evil things. I sensed it or should have. But I was bogged down in a stupor of depression and despair. So maybe I just chose not to see what became so clear in retrospect. I hunkered down and waited for the day to come. Her plans were made. And she told me. All was set. She would leave in March.

March. The date seemed far away yet so close. As the days counted down to D-Day, I felt it in the distance like some huge, looming storm. Approaching slowly, moving toward me inexorably, relentlessly.

I feared growing old alone.

We got along, mostly. Like I said. There was one major fight, in early January. It came at us on a Saturday afternoon. She was packing her things in plastic storage containers she had bought at Walmart. I paced about the house, perturbed. I muttered some comment about how it wasn't going to work, her moving all the way out west like that.

My words were not well received. She confronted me, her face contorted with rage. "Stop it right now," she screamed. "All you do is walk around saying smug, stupid things. Stop it." Tears of frustration rolled down her cheeks.

I walked into the living room and sat on the couch, shaking. She raged on. I waited until the tirade subsided. "You are my wife, and I love you," I said dully. "What am I supposed to do, just sit around and watch you leave? We are married. You are my wife. I am your husband. To me, that means something."

We both trembled with tension and anger and stress. She struggled to control herself. "You've known I'm leaving," she said, more calmly. "And you haven't done anything to stop it. Now all of a sudden you act like you don't want me to go."

"I've never wanted you to go," I retorted. "You know that. You're the one who's leaving. I'm not."

She looked at me, and the rage seemed to drain from her. She spoke my name. This was unusual. We rarely addressed each other by name anymore.

"Ira, your heart left this marriage a long time ago," she said.

D-Day minus one. A Wednesday. I went to work as usual, then to the gym. Tried to approach the day as normally as possible. My great fear was that I would break down as she was leaving. I dreaded the actual moment.

She would leave early the next morning. I had arranged to take the day off from work. I would go work out at the gym, then meet a close friend at noon. At a park for a few hours, just to talk it out and help me get through that fateful day.

She had packed all her things. I helped her carry the plastic storage boxes to the garage, where they would stay until she could come and retrieve them. All the stuff she would take with her was packed in suitcases and bags and boxes.

Evening came and darkness fell. Her car was parked outside, at the end of the short walkway. Pointed toward the road.

Around nine p.m., she was ready to load. I lugged out the large suitcase and placed it in the trunk. Then stuffed in boxes and bags and jammed the trunk lid down. Then I crammed the back seat with boxes and bags until it was full.

We chatted amiably. It felt strange. Surreal. But I held up. I knew that when she drove away the next morning, she would never return.

We talked. I asked her to text me when she arrived at her destination. So I'd know she was safe. She said she would. We went to bed late, after eleven o'clock. She gave me half an Ambien so I could sleep and took the other half herself. Mercifully, we both fell asleep in minutes.

We slept through the night. The clattering alarm roused us. I awoke. And realized the date was here. The date that had loomed so fearfully in my mind for so long.

She got up, and I heard her puttering around in the kitchen and the bathroom. Getting ready to leave our home. I lay there in bed. Awake. And numb.

The final moment. She walked through the bedroom doorway. "I'm ready," she said.

"Take care" was all I could think to say. That was all. Nothing profound.

She approached me and stood by the side of the bed. Leaned above me. Placed her arm around me. Said a short prayer. For traveling safety. For herself. For strength. For me. I said nothing. She walked out of the bedroom. The kitchen light went dark. I heard the porch door shutting softly. And then she was gone. I lay there, but sleep did not come again.

After a while, I got up. Took a shower. Got dressed. An evil pulse throbbed silently through the house, a harbinger of the brutal truths that would emerge in the coming months. The eastern sky shimmered with the brilliant hues of dawn. The day broke. It would be clear and sunny.

It was March. The cruelest month.

I walked outside alone to face the world.

———

I muddled through, those first few months. Ellen moved to a faraway city out west. I stumbled along at home. And that first summer, she filed the divorce papers from where she was. I didn't fight anything. I signed where I needed to sign and sent the papers back. And I will say this. It was a numbing and painful time. But through all that, our divorce could not have been more amicable than it was. We never even hired any lawyers at all. Just signed an agreement written up by an attorney friend of mine. We listed her stuff and listed mine. Before leaving, she had lugged in some big old tubs and loaded them with her things, and I had carried the tubs out to the garage and stacked them there against the wall. There they remained for many years, and I never had a problem with any of all that. There were a few pieces of furniture, too, that stayed. And I was OK with that as well. It was pretty strange, how relaxed it all came down in some ways. It really was.

The divorce got finalized that fall, in November of 2007. It was kind of funny how that happened. From here, any-way, it was. Back then, it wasn't. I had gotten the official notice. On such and such a day, at four thirty p.m. my time, the judge would call me from the bench. And we'd go through with the hearing. I dreaded the moment, but still, you just walk forward in a time like that. That's all you can do. The day came. Four thirty came. No phone call. Then it was closing time at the office, five o'clock. I got into my truck and headed for home. Over the mountain. And as I approached the little town of White Horse, sure enough, my cell phone rang. A blocked number. I couldn't see where it was coming from. I answered. "Hello."

An authoritative female voice. "Is this Ira Wagler?"

I hedged. "Depends on who's asking."

"This is Judge [I don't remember her name]," she said. "Is this Ira Wagler? Please identify yourself."

I was done hedging. "It is," I said. I was driving right by the fire station, so I pulled in and parked. And we proceeded with the hearing. I answered a few questions, and I heard Ellen's voice answering the same questions on the other end. It was all pretty laid back.

And after ten minutes or so, the judge was done. "I hereby declare you divorced," she proclaimed. And then it was over. I hung up and just sat there for a moment.

It felt so very strange. I remember thinking, *I'm divorced*. Then, before driving on, I called my brother, Stephen. "I just got divorced in the parking lot of the White Horse Fire Station," I told him. Stephen had known it was coming, but he was just silent for a moment. He said something then, I don't remember what. And I told him, "I'm sure it's probably the first time in history that anyone got divorced in the parking lot of a fire station." We both chuckled. It was funny, when you thought about it. And then I drove on out toward home.

THE LONG GOOD-BYE

SHE WAS BEDRIDDEN now, mostly, they told me. She'd stay that way all the time, they told me, too. Except they got her up every day, for at least a little while. Sat her in a chair so her body position changed. And so the blood could flow. Ate, because they fed her. She didn't know a whole lot, if anything, about what was going on around her. Except she smiled sometimes, as if she grasped a bit of it. But then she reclined back on the bed and fell asleep. And she slept and slept. Through the night, into the next day. And they did it all over again. Woke her. Got her up. Cleaned her. Then fed her as a baby is fed. One spoonful at a time. Then she'd sit for a while in her wheelchair, maybe. But always, soon, back to bed. In 2012, that was the state of my mother's long, helpless descent into the cruel and fading twilight that is Alzheimer's.

We had noticed the first little bumps in her memory about a dozen years before. You can't ever precisely pinpoint the onset of Alzheimer's, not when it's coming at you, because it comes at you slow. An aberration, at first. A flash of anger so far out of character that you flinch back. What was that? Where did that come from? That's not who you are. And that's how it was with Mom. We looked back from that point and saw the first few times. Her words were hurtful to the person she spoke to. That could not have been my mother speaking. But she said the words, in all their savage meaning.

Her condition didn't deteriorate that fast, really. But it was steady. And by around 2004, we spoke the dreadful word in our family. Alzheimer's. Mom was coming down with it. I don't really remember how I felt. Just a sense of foreboding, I think, along with a vague and desperate hope that she wouldn't linger for years and years in that condition. Not like her older sister Mary, who had silently suffered in a hollow shell for ten years.

They lived in Bloomfield, Iowa, then, she and Dad. In a cozy little *Daudy* house on my brother Joseph's farm. Their house was connected to his by a walkway. Joseph had moved from his old home north of West Grove and bought Gid Yutzy's dilapidated old farm along Drakesville Road at public auction. A perfect place for his metal-sales business. Two miles south of Drakesville. Right in the center of the community, along a paved road.

And they settled in their little house, she and Dad. Back then she still cooked on her wood-burning kitchen stove. And on the kerosene stove in summer. Mostly did well getting the meals together. The rhythm of her life was so ingrained that she walked her daily steps from habit. At that time, she kept a little flock of chickens in a tiny run-down wooden shack.

She walked out every day, rain or snow or shine, to feed them, talk to them, and gather the eggs. Fussed when the hens came up one egg short. Which one wasn't feeling well? She'd have to look into it. Take care of the matter. And the chickens clucked and came running when she called. She smiled and chattered at them. "Here's your feed for today. Eat well now, and lay me lots of eggs."

And it seemed like that was where they would end their days in peace, she and Dad. Right there in the cozy *Daudy* house in Bloomfield. Sure, most of the family had scattered now, moved out. Only two of their sons and their wives remained in Bloomfield. Joseph and Iva. And Titus and Ruth, a mile or so south and west.

And I remember the last time we were there, in that house, Ellen and me. During the winter of 2006–2007. I'm not sure exactly of the date. We knew we didn't have long to be together anymore, so we made one last trip home together to see Dad and Mom. The roads were sheets of ice when we arrived. I remember the bleak, dreary day, how the biting sleet swept sideways from the sky. The kitchen stove crackled, the little house was almost uncomfortably warm. Mom met us, smiling. Dad was sitting in the living room, pounding away at his typewriter. He got up to shake hands, then folded his arms, and he and I sat down to visit.

Mom welcomed us both. Ellen sat there in the kitchen with her, drinking coffee, and the two of them just chatted right along in Pennsylvania Dutch. Mom always completely accepted Ellen. I guess Dad did, too, after we were married. It never was Mom who wouldn't come to the wedding. That was Dad, all the way. And on this day, Mom had a little gift. A little white home-sewn apron. For Ellen to wear when she was cooking, Mom said. And I watched them and grieved quietly in my heart. The two of them together, laughing and talking. I knew this would be the last time. It was.

Mom went downhill rapidly in 2007, mostly mentally, but physically, too. She was still active, though, still absorbed in her daily household work. That was all she ever knew, and even though her mind was receding, her body stayed on autopilot.

In some ways, her condition was a blessing for me, I suppose. That spring, my marriage fell apart, and my world imploded around me. I hunkered down in the storm. All my siblings and even my father quietly offered support such as I had not expected and had never known before. But they never told Mom. She never had to endure or absorb the knowledge that her son had messed up his life to such a low point. And that he now was slogging down a tough, weary road. I'm glad she didn't know. But with that blissful blessing of ignorance also came a sorrow, for me, a few years later. She never knew that I wrote of her, told of her world as it was, and so much of what she had endured. She never knew that I dedicated my first book to her.

We gathered around her when we could, her children. At weddings and funerals, and sometimes over Christmas. And right up until the summer of 2012, she always recognized us and spoke our names. She wasn't there much in any other way, but she knew her children. And with the passing of each month, it seemed, she sank ever farther into a world we cannot know, a world from which no one has ever returned to tell of how it was.

I remember the early 1990s, when Nathan and I headed home to Bloomfield every year at Christmastime. How Mom always welcomed us, excited and smiling. Her boys were home. And then, a few days later, as our departure loomed, how she smiled still. Bravely. The sadness shone from her eyes. "Good-bye," she said with forced cheer. "Good-bye. Drive carefully and take care. Come home again." And she always pressed some little gift into our hands.

And we spoke awkwardly to her. "Good-bye, Mom. We will." We never hugged, because the Amish don't hug, mostly. At least not in any world I had seen up until that time.

As she slowly sank into the darkness, I wished there were a way to say good-bye to her one more time like that. Not as I was leaving her. But as she was leaving us on the final leg of her journey home.

I'd like to go back and say good-bye to her one more time like that. This time, I would hug her.

STONE ANGEL REDUX

MAYBE IT WAS subconscious, the reason I bought that little stone angel back in late 2006, just before Ellen left. Maybe, too, it was a silent appeal to God for help. I don't know. I do know that the angel was brought home and set up outside in the garden. Looking at our house. Lifting its tiny stone hands in prayer for me and my wife. The angel's prayers didn't help, apparently, at least not in any immediate way. Quite the opposite, I'd say. Instead of peace, there came turmoil.

Our world blew up in a spectacular fiery crash. Just blew into smithereens. I hunkered down, all alone, in the house we had bought together and lived in together for seven years. I was too shell-shocked, probably, to do much else. But I instinctively held on to what I knew I would not do. I would not leave my home. I would stay here. By myself, if that was what it took. I hunkered down, didn't talk to a lot of people. Just a few close friends, mostly people at work. And then, for the first time in my life, I did what I had never done before in any serious manner. I began to write.

I never told the neighbors what had happened. They had eyes, I figured, to see something drastic had come down. And from what they saw, they must have wondered if anyone lived in the house anymore. I disappeared early every morning. Got back home every evening around seven or so. My truck parked out back, that and the lights burning late into the night as I wrote and wrote, those were pretty much the only signs that the place was even inhabited. And it wasn't that I couldn't have told them, couldn't have faced them. I just didn't feel like it. And so I didn't.

And that spring, Ellen's little garden lay fallow. It never got tilled or planted. The flower beds, too, all nicely mulched the year before, were simply ignored. Giant weeds sprouted everywhere and overwhelmed the flowers that had been planted. And again, it wasn't that I couldn't have taken care of things, made the place look good. It wasn't that I wanted anything to look bad. It was just that it all didn't matter that much to me. I existed. Went to work every morning. From there, to the gym. And from the gym to home. A routine, focused cycle. That was me at that time. And every night, I sat at my computer, and the words poured forth in great torrents.

And that summer, the weeds grew wild and free in the garden. The shrub where the angel stood grew out, too, extended its branches. And sometime during that summer, the angel just disappeared from sight. Under the embracing darkness of the branches of the shrub tree. And behind the weeds that grew wild. I looked now and then but thought little of it. It wasn't that I didn't want to see my little stone angel friend. It was just that I didn't care enough to make it happen. And it languished there unseen all that year, into the fall and winter.

A year passed. Then two. I kept on writing and writing. My marriage exploding had been the catalyst, the event that pushed me out, that made me write my voice for the first time ever, in my life. The trigger.

It was a brutal and bitter place to find my writing voice. I guess you don't get to choose when something happens organically on its own like that. It just is what it is, and gets here when it gets here. I hunkered down in those early years and spoke from deep pits of darkness and pain such as I had never seen before and have not seen since.

And just throwing my stuff out on my blog. Eventually, my voice calmed a great deal, and I settled in. Began to write about a whole lot of things. Stories from my childhood. This and that, from where I was. This was a new place in my life. And I walked it free. Spoke it as I saw it, whatever I wrote about. From where I was, and from my heart. And the angel remained standing there, completely obscured by branches and brambles and weeds, through all that time.

As you look back from where you are after you cross it, a valley often seems a little deeper and a little more intimidating than it actually was, I think. I mean, sure, it was tough, that road. No way I'd ever want to go back to that place. Not ever. And sure, it shook up a lot of things

I thought I knew. But still, when you're in a place like that, you do what you know in the moment. You plug along. You deal with all the crap, all the gripping pain. But mostly, you keep walking. And eventually you get through it. That's what I can say from where I am today, looking back.

And the Lord looked down upon me and smiled. He really did. I kept on writing. And He blessed my efforts. First, with a large readership for my blog. And eventually, someone knew someone who knew an agent and notified him. That agent, Chip MacGregor, contacted me. I signed up. He took my stuff and shopped it around. And things moved right along, and one evening Chip emailed me with the news. He got me an offer from Tyndale House. For a book.

I took the offer, of course. Signed the contract they sent me. And soon enough, a nice little check arrived in the mail. A small down payment for the book. Half up front, half when it was done. I accepted the check gratefully. And I knew what needed to be done. The house. It needed new windows. Those had never been replaced. Every time a cold winter wind blew, you could feel the breeze inside from five feet away. But I wouldn't do them all at once, I figured. That would take more money than the check was made out for. I'd do half the house first. The west and north sides. Upstairs and downstairs. I contacted an Amish contractor. And he came out and gave me a quote. Decent price. "Go ahead," I told him.

And his crew came out that summer. And for the first time since living here alone, I made improvements to my home. The neighbors stared. Ira is getting his house worked on. What's the world coming to? Oh well. His yard still looks pretty scraggly, though. And things didn't change at all on the outside, on the grounds. The shrub tree by the shop still grew unchecked. And covered now with clogging vines. The weeds stood tall around the brush pile that had accumulated in what once was a rich and fertile little garden. And the stone angel stood with clasped and praying hands, completely out of sight.

Late that year, in 2010, I finished the manuscript. Well, I finished the raw mass of words that made up my manuscript. Pages and pages, with no chapter breaks, even, in much of it. The Tyndale people sorted it out from there. And the second check arrived. I had finished. And the next spring, I called the Amish contractor back. The windows on the south and east sides. I needed those replaced. The man smiled and wrote up a quote. I signed it and gave him a check. And his crew came right on in and worked its magic. The neighbors stared some more at the new windows in my house. Now, when is he gonna do something about that yard? And the stone angel remained where it had stood since the day I bought it. Still out of sight.

And the book took off and did what it did. *Growing Up Amish*. From a writer's perspective, you have to believe you got what it takes, to even throw your stuff out there to start with. But still, when it really does take off like that, it's a little freaky. And humbling. And that first year, some very nice checks came rolling in. I had to sit down when the first one arrived. And once again, I thought of my house.

The mortar between the bricks. That should be re-placed. Around here, they call that repointing. It's called tuck-pointing in other parts of the country. I knew it had to be done. And I knew it was an expensive process. From the labor involved, mostly. They have to grind out the old mortar so the new mortar can be applied. It's a dirty, grimy, endless job.

A year after I'd gotten married, I'd left my attorney job. Gone to work at a building-supply business. And now, being in the trade, I had the contacts. I knew whom to talk to. And I did. Called the guy, earlier that year, which was 2013. "Hey, I'm heading out traveling in the first half of May. I need a quote to get my house repointed. And I'd like it done when I'm gone." It was an Amish guy, of course. I've known him for years, he's an Eagles fan. I always rib him about that. "Thugs, the Eagles are," I tell him. And he claims a Jets fan has nothing to say about all that. And he stopped by and measured up the place. They could do it for this price. And yes, they could do it while I was gone. I looked at the quote and recoiled a bit. Hard-earned money, just going out the window like that. It galled me.

In the meantime, things were shaking on other fronts that year. In March, I rented the upstairs apartment to a new tenant. It had stood empty for more than two years. And it was in sad disrepair. The new tenant was "new" in a lot of ways. An older guy, separated from his wife after a few dozen years of marriage. And it didn't take long after he got here. The man was a restless fixer-upper. Some-thing my place desperately needed. "Well," he'd tell me.

"I saw this needed painting. I saw where this screw was loose on the gutters on your house. I stopped by the hardware store and picked up a few things I needed. And I fixed it."

I gaped at him and marveled. And I told him, "Bring me your receipts, and keep track of your time. I'll pay you for what you do."

He's the best tenant I've ever had, hands down. He's honest, and he treats me right. He works with his hands to make the things around him more beautiful. And he always pays the rent on time, pays it early, even. I don't know if he even goes to church. I think not, but I never asked him. What am I going to say? He's lived here in Lancaster County around "Christians" all his life. He knows them, he knows who they are, from how they live and how they treat him. And if he doesn't go to church at his age, I figure he has his reasons. Maybe he'll tell me about it someday.

And before I left on my travels that summer, I told him, "The crew will be here to repoint the house while I'm gone." He seemed to think that was a very good plan indeed. And two weeks later, as my truck swept around the corner late that night, getting home, I saw it had been done. Even in the dark, the bright new mortar glinted in the headlights. The boys had done it. The next morning, I got up and walked out to look at my house in daylight. It was just beautiful, it looked new, almost. The boys had done it right.

One day that summer, we stood out on the back side of the house, where I park my truck, just talking. The tenant said something about how nice it would be to get those flower beds cleaned up around the house. And mulched. He knew people who would do it for a reasonable price, he claimed. "Sure," I said. "And while they're at it, I need to get the branches trimmed on this big old pine tree. They hang down so low, they scrape my truck every time I drive out. And this old brush pile," I said, pointing to where the garden used to be. "It's pretty ugly. I need someone to clean it all up."

And the neighbors must have gaped some more as his friends converged on the place. The painters came and power-washed the old paint on the porch. Then they left and came back and started painting. By hand. The floor a light gray. White pillars and railings. And the classic sky blue on the ceiling. They puttered about when they could fit it in, a few hours here, a few hours there. Which I didn't mind at all. And the next Saturday morning, as I left to run some errands, two more of my tenant's buddies had parked their truck and trailer and were cleaning up the brush pile. I was in and out a few times. They plugged away. And I left that afternoon again, for a few hours. I returned later, around six or so. Pulled into my drive. And I looked out to the garage and just stared.

The brush pile had been removed completely. The weeds whacked down. The shrub tree trimmed back. All the crawly vines removed. And there in plain sight for the first time since Ellen had left, the little white angel stood, revealed to all the world. It stood, wings folded, hands clasped, frozen in prayer. And it took my breath away.

I stood there and absorbed the setting. And a few minutes later, the tenant came strolling by. We stood around and talked, and I told him the story of the angel. What was going on back in those dark days when I bought it. How I had set it there, right where it stood. And how it had remained there, hidden, since almost the day I'd brought it home. "Of all the things that you made happen here, this one is the most important," I told him. "That angel symbolizes a lot of things. Believe me. A lot of things."

And I told him something more. "Thank you. Thank you for stepping in and getting this stuff done. You have been nothing but a blessing to me from the day you walked through my door." He smiled his quiet smile and beamed.

The stone angel stands now, looking to the south, lifting its tiny hands as if praying for a shield of protection over my home. It stands there, right where I placed it when I bought it. Right where it has always stood for years, covered by leaves and brambles and vines and weeds. For most of those years, you just couldn't see it, because it was too much of a reminder of all that hard stuff from the past.

The thing is, I'm not sure when I ever would have dredged up the courage or the energy to uncover that angel, had the right person not showed up to nudge me through that door and get it done. And you see it, when it happens in real life, you see a path to freedom you could not find before on your own. It took a flawed man with a broken past, it took such a man to wander through and stop in for a while. And he didn't even realize what all was going on, but he's the one who made the little stone angel now stand as it was always meant to stand. In the open, and freely visible to all who pass by.

I'm just grateful that he showed up. And that he got here right on time.

RETURNING TO
MY FATHER

IN THE SUMMER of 2013, I drove up to see my parents. It would be the last time I saw Mom alive. That Friday afternoon, I pulled into the town of Aylmer, Ontario. That's where my parents had moved back to a few years before, after Mom started slipping mentally. To Aylmer, where they lived in a tiny little *Daudy* house at my oldest sister Rosemary's home. Aylmer, the place where I had been born and raised. The town was just impossibly small, from the great metropolis I'd remembered as a child. A bare little town, with a little row of shops huddled forlornly around a stoplight at a crossroad. I passed through the light and headed on out west toward Saint Thomas.

Saint Thomas is a bigger place than Aylmer. I remember the name from my childhood, but I don't remember the town. Because it was out there, just a bit outside the edges of my world. And I was going there now to find a motel room. I'd looked it up on the web, and I knew there was a good selection. And sure enough, right there on the east side of town as I approached was a brand-new Comfort Inn. I've seen some trashy Comfort Inns. This wasn't one. I pulled in and chatted with the clerk, a nice lady. "I'm here from Pennsylvania, to see family," I told her. And I booked a room for two nights. It was late afternoon, past five. I carried in my bag and settled in a bit, then headed out to my sister Rosemary's farm to hang out for the evening.

I headed back east to Aylmer, then down the main road through the community. It was barely recognizable as the place I'd known as a child all those years ago. Way more built up, with a lot more Amish homes scattered along the way. No one knew me or knew I was there. I passed through the heart of the settlement, then took a left on the road to my sister Rosemary's home farm. They'd be looking for me. I pulled in and walked into her home.

She smiled and welcomed me. "I'm so glad you came," she said.

"Yeah, me too," I said. And we just sat there and caught up. I hadn't seen her since the previous summer, when I went up to see Mom.

"Joe will be home soon," she said. "Just stay here for supper, then you can go over to see Dad for the evening."

So that's what I did. Mom was not feeling well, Rosemary told me. She had a fever now, for the second day. The nurse was stopping by that evening to check it out. Soon Rosemary's husband, Joe, arrived home from Tillsonburg, where he had been peddling strawberries door to door. Some things never change. I used to do that as a child. And we sat down at their little table to eat. A simple meal. Soup and homemade sausage. Homemade stuffed sausage, hickory smoked, just like we used to have way back. Rosemary has kept the tradition, and to me, there is no better sausage anywhere than the stuff I grew up with.

After supper, we walked over to the little house where my parents lived. It was a tiny place, a shack, really, probably twenty feet wide and maybe thirty feet long. A nice clean place with a tiny kitchen, a bedroom, and a little office in the corner where Dad wrote. And he was sitting there, at his typewriter. He heard us walking in and looked up.

"Hi, Dad," I said. He was old, approaching ninety-two. But he was there. You could see his concentration when he listened to you talk. He smiled at me, and we shook hands.

"Well, you made it," he said. His voice was cracked now. And we went through our normal little routine, our normal little dance. "How was the trip?" he asked.

"Oh, good," I said. "I left Pennsylvania this morning. It's a long old drag up here, but I made pretty good time."

"Where are you staying?" he asked.

"I got a motel room in Saint Thomas," I told him. As we talked, Rosemary slipped into the bedroom, where Mom was. I walked in behind her. And there she lay. Curled up. Unaware.

"She has a fever," Rosemary told me again. And I bent down close to my mother's wrinkled face.

"Mom. It's me. Ira." There was no response, of course.

Dad came stumping into the kitchen then, and I sat down with him to visit. We chatted about this and that. And he asked me then, "How many copies of your book have sold?"

"Oh, right at 140,000," I said. I wasn't sure. Last I'd heard from the Tyndale people, it was in the 130,000s and counting. But that was a while ago. So I figured it was safe to slip it up there to the next level.

He grappled a bit with that figure. "How many?"

"140,000 copies," I said again. He seemed impressed.

Then five minutes later, he asked again. "How many copies?" And I told him again. Seemed like he had to hear the number a few times to grasp it. Or to make sure he hadn't heard wrong.

And we sat there and talked, the two of us, and it was good. After a bit, the nurse stopped in to see Mom. She disappeared with Rosemary into the bedroom. Ten minutes later, she emerged. "Her vital signs are all strong," the nurse said. "She has constipation." And she and Rosemary talked about what to do about that.

The evening was moving right along. It was soon time for me to head to the motel. And I told Dad, "I'm here to see you. What do you want to do tomorrow? Do you want to go somewhere, to see someone, to visit?" And I could see the wheels turning in his head. He knew I knew that he wouldn't ride with me in my car. He never has. His calculations led to the only place they could.

And he asked, looking at me kind of sideways, "Well, will you drive with me in my buggy?"

"Sure," I said. "If your horse is safe."

He laughed. "Oh, yes, my horse is an old plug."

"All right," I said. "That'll work. Maybe we can go see David Luthy at his historical library. I haven't been there in a lot of years." Dad agreed. That would be fine. He seemed a little astounded that I'd ride with him in the buggy. "It's not a big deal," I said. "I came to see you, and we'll go do what you want." I said good night then and headed back to Saint Thomas and my room.

The next morning around nine I drove out to the farm. Stopped in Aylmer at Tim Hortons and bought coffee to drink and a box of a dozen doughnuts to take out with me. Tim Hortons is a Canadian phenomenon. Every little burg has one. And they serve some of the better doughnuts I've ever tasted. Way better than the ones at Dunkin'. And their coffee, too, is just quality. I wish that chain would open more stores in the US. Anyway, out I drove into the beautiful cloudless day. All day, I'd spend all day out there. Mostly with Dad, but I'd spend some time with Rosemary and her family, too.

I arrived and carried the box of doughnuts into the house. Rosemary smiled her thanks. Her daughter Edna was flitting about, working this and that. "Dad and I are leaving for David Luthy's in his buggy," I told her. "Can someone get the horse hitched up? We need to leave around ten or a little after. I'll drive the horse, but I want nothing to do with going to the barn or hitching him up."

Edna laughed and disappeared. Ten minutes later, she returned. "The horse is hitched up and tied up, out by the rail," she said. "Ready for you and Daudy anytime."

"Thanks," I said. "I'll go over and chat with him now. We'll leave soon." And I walked over to Dad's little house. He was in his office. I sat in the chair across from his desk, and we talked. "Ready to go soon?" I asked.

In the bedroom next door, I heard voices. Rosemary was getting Mom up for a few hours. A neighbor lady was there to help. They'd get her up in her wheelchair so the pressure points on her body wouldn't cause bedsores. And she'd sit there and recline and mostly sleep. A few minutes later, they wheeled her out into the kitchen. I heard Rosemary talking to her. "Ira is here," Rosemary said. "He came to see you and Dad."

And I heard the murmur of her voice, soft but very clear, in the only lucid moment she had while I was there. "You mean our Ira?" she asked.

"Yes, our Ira," Rosemary answered.

And I stepped out to greet her. "Mom, it's me." But in that instant, she was gone again.

"She knew there for a second you were here," Rosemary said. "But she's gone again."

"Yeah, I know," I answered. "I heard her. I'm grateful for that."

"The horse is hitched up and ready," I told Dad. "We need to leave soon. We have to be back for dinner [noon meal]." He was all hyped up and ready. Grabbed his big old black hat and put it on. We walked out to where the horse was tied up. He hobbled slowly, and I walked slowly. We came up to his buggy, specially built for him. It was in the old classic Aylmer style, with rubber-tired wheels. But they'd set it down lower, somehow. It sat close to the ground, so it was easier for him to get in and out. I untied the horse and took the reins. Backed him up a bit, then turned out onto the lane. And headed out to the road. There I stopped and looked both ways for traffic. I wasn't feeling all that safe right at that moment, I have to say. Those buggies just aren't safe on the roads. Nothing was coming, so I pulled on the right rein and clucked. The horse, whose name escapes me, lumbered out and down the road. And we were off.

It had been a lot of years since I rode with my father in a buggy. Decades, probably. Maybe longer. Somewhere in there, I'm sure I had since I was a child. I just couldn't remember when. We didn't have far to go. A mile, maybe. And we just chatted right along as the buggy quietly rolled along on rubber-tired wheels. "Junior lives here now, with his family," Dad said as we passed the old Jake Eicher place. "He had some kind of accident a few years ago, crushed his heel. They have a real nice family." We passed Pathway Publishers on the left. Then right at the corner and on past a few more homes and the old schoolhouse where I went for first grade. Well, those grounds. They tore the old schoolhouse down years ago and built a new one. But the old pump still sits there, right where it was. And the swing set. Still the same one.

Then we arrived at David Luthy's place. At that time the preeminent Amish historian in the world, David Luthy had assembled one of the world's more notable collections of old books and other paraphernalia that were Amish family heirlooms. He has written extensively for *Family Life* over the decades. Real research is what he does. Historical articles, a great many of which detail and describe failed Amish communities through the years. And it was a special thing, to have an inside track to his library. It's not open to the public. You have to have an appointment, and even then you still might not be able to get in, depending on who you are. That's how hard it is to get in there. But I was with Dad. He can get in anytime, almost. And I could get in with him.

David greeted us. He was there in his office, typing away. He was older now, his long magnificent beard was no longer dark, but gray. His wife, Mary, rushed out from the house, smiling. She welcomed me. They'd known me as a child. And we walked to a back room and sat around a table. For more than an hour, David told me fascinating tale after fascinating tale of his library, and about some of his acquisitions. He unveiled and showed me an exact replica of an original Gutenberg Bible, complete with gold-plated pages and illustrations. We examined ancient copies of *Martyrs Mirror* and *Ausbund*. David talked and talked. Just before noon, Dad and I got up to leave. We walked out to his low-slung buggy, and he stepped in. I untied the horse and stepped in, too. Then we were off, back to Rosemary's house and dinner.

Things were bustling at the farm when we got back. It had been wet for weeks, and Lester, Rosemary's married son who farmed the homeplace, had hay down in the fields. It had been rained on to where it was pretty much ruined, he told me. But he figured he could bale it and get it out of his field late that afternoon. It was junk, but he had to get it off the field so the next cutting could grow. I spent a few hours at Rosemary's home, while Dad returned to his desk and his writing. And they stopped by to see me for a few minutes, a few of my nieces and nephews, Rosemary's children. Her oldest daughter, Eunice, came with a couple of her daughters. Her younger son, Philip, and his wife stopped by early that evening.

And then, around five or so, I wandered over to see Dad again. He was sitting at his desk, typing away. They'd gotten rid of his old manual model. Probably ran out of parts. It was an electric typewriter he used now, adapted to a twelve-volt battery. It hardly made any noise. Sure didn't clatter and clack and ding, like the one I remembered him using. He stopped typing and leaned back in his chair. And the two of us just talked.

We chatted for a while about this and that. And I knew he wouldn't bring it up. So I asked him, right out, "What did you think of the book?"

And he leaned back some more and smiled self-consciously. "Well." And he sat there a bit. "I guess I'd ask this: What do you think the world thinks about the Amish and about me?"

So that was it? That was his sorrow? I chose my words carefully. And I told him, "They will think you are a talented and driven man who got a lot accomplished in your life as an Amish person," I said. "And they will know you were flawed. But we are all flawed. All of us. You are. I am. It doesn't make any sense to pretend we're not."

Maybe he grasped that. Maybe not. I think he did, a little. And then he talked some more. "People have told me they were impressed, and I agree," he said. "You tried, you really tried to make it work. I'll give you that. You came back and tried again and again." That was pretty huge, to hear him say such a thing. To recognize that. But then he balanced it out. "I still think it was a mistake to hang around that café so much," he said. And he talked some more about this scene and that. "You sure got it right about your horse," he said. "That's exactly as I remember it. I remember how beaten down you were when your horse died. And how I offered to buy you another one. But you wouldn't take it. I never could quite understand why."

"I was depressed," I said. "I just needed to get out. I knew I couldn't make it. That's why I turned down your offer." He seemed to absorb that. And we talked a bit more. I wanted to mention a few other things from the book to get his thoughts. I just didn't get it all done. And then he talked about Sam Johnson. Dad seemed to understand why Sam had cut me off. And he approved of it. Sam had had to cut me off, because I hadn't stayed. "OK," I said. "Doesn't make much sense to me, but if that's how it had to be, then that's how it had to be."

And he talked again about Sarah, too, and how I'd wronged her. "Yes," I said. "I did. I did wrong her, very much so. I made that pretty clear, I think. Like I said, we're all flawed. I certainly am. But I just tried to tell the story. That's the only way to write a story. Tell it like it was. Be honest about who you were when you tell it. And who you are now."

Rosemary clattered into the kitchen then, carrying a large tray. Food for our supper. "The men are out baling hay, so we won't eat until later," she told us. "So I brought your supper. Come to the table and eat."

Dad and I got up and walked to the kitchen. I sat down. He paused where Mom was sitting a few feet away, napping. He spoke to her, some lighthearted question.

"Every day, I try to say something that makes her smile," he said. And then he stumped over to the little table and took his seat.

This is a remarkable moment, I thought. Not that long ago, he wouldn't sit with me at any table. He wouldn't eat with me. Because he was shunning me. I had told him back then, "I'm not excommunicated." The Goshen Amish church where I left was more progressive. And I wasn't excommunicated. Well, I was, but after I joined the Mennonite church in Daviess, they lifted it. Made it like it never was. And I told Dad that. But he'd still shun me, he told me, because he felt like that was the right thing to do. And he did. Back then. For a lot of years.

But not now. I uncovered the dishes on the tray. Meat, chips, lettuce, freshly chopped tomatoes, and cheese. And dressing. "A taco salad," I said.

Dad pulled up his chair then, and we paused and bowed our heads. I wondered if he'd pray aloud. He used to, years back. And sure enough, he spoke it. The meal-blessing prayer. In his cracked voice, with that old rhythm he always had. *"Alle Augen worten auf Dich, oh Herr, denn Du gibst Ihn Ihre Speise zu Seiner Zeit..."* (The eyes of all wait upon thee, and thou givest them their meat in due season...Psalm 145:15). I sat there and drank it in. He finished the prayer, and we took the food on our plates and ate. Just the two of us together, at that little table in that little room in that little house.

After the meal, I sat with Dad in his office, and we just talked. He was working on his own memoir. Two binders of notes were spread out beside his typewriter. Some months before, he had sent a few dozen pages of the first draft to all his children. So we could check it out. "I liked it," I told him. "I learned things I never knew before about you. Keep it up. Keep writing. I want to read what you have to say. I liked it a lot. Don't worry about the moral lessons, though, in your story. Just write it. Trust your readers. And respect them. If there's lessons to be learned, they'll pick those up on their own. You don't need to tell them."

He pondered that a bit. I'm not sure he quite grasped what I was trying to say, because he never wrote like that. Just the story. He pretty much always had an explicit lesson poked in there somewhere at the end. Because that was how he wrote. We sat there, and I looked at him from across the desk as the sun slanted to the west.

Later that night, after I returned to my motel room and darkness closed in, I thought about it. The whole day. The time I'd spent with Dad. Especially our meal together at the little table. And hearing him pray that prayer, that was a special thing. It was a gift, all of it, every minute of this day. And at that moment, I saw it in my mind, as clearly as if I were standing back there, what was going on about now in the little house where my parents lived.

Mom was in bed for the night. They'd tucked her in earlier. And Dad, well, Dad was doing what he did almost every evening. Sitting in his office, pounding away at his typewriter. Except in his old age, he shut down early. He couldn't stay up half the night. Not like he used to. He was too old. And he was just too tired, he simply didn't have it in him anymore. And now he was getting up to get ready for bed. He carried the lamp into the kitchen and set it on the table. Opened the bedroom door so Mom could hear. And then he knelt there by a chair.

And in a cracked and faltering voice, still laced with remnants of the comforting rhythmic flow his children have always known and will always remember, he prayed that beautiful old High German evening prayer by heart. Beautiful, is what all those old formal German prayers are. Just breathtakingly beautiful. And he spoke it, the prayer for this evening. Thanking God for His love and the gift of salvation. Thanking God for all His blessings. Asking the Lord to lift His benevolent hand of protection over him and his family, those he loved. All alone now, he prayed every morning as the day broke. And every evening after the sun had set.

Kneeling there, in the bleakness of his bare surroundings, he prayed for all his family. He prayed for Mom. For his children and his children's children. Wherever they were scattered on the whole earth. And the children still to come, he prayed for them, too, the generations beyond. He prayed for all of them in the only way he knew how. Just like he always had.

REUBEN AND ME

THERE'S AN OLD friend in my life. His name is Reuben. We've known each other all our lives. We were pretty much best friends, in all that time. I mean, from back when we were kids. And a number of years back, he made some very, very bad choices. He chose to walk down some real hard roads. He made some destructive, destructive decisions. And his world blew up. Just blew up into smithereens, like mine did. He chose to leave his wife and family for an idol. He did that. Walked away from his family. And from where I was at that time, well, he chose to leave all we had known as old friends for an idol, too. And we were totally estranged, he and I, for a few years.

I guess it needs to be said why. This is why. My marriage to Ellen was failing, all on its own. It would have failed, anyway. Reuben kind of hastened the inevitable by having an affair with my wife. My eyes were open. I should have known. But I didn't. Some places, your mind just won't go. Refuses to go. It all came out, brilliantly clear, after

Ellen left our home. She and Reuben were figuring to be together in the future. The moves he made, those were all geared to that one disastrous goal. It was a brutal blow, and it was a brutal betrayal. From both of them.

At the time, I wrote savagely at Reuben, mostly on my blog. I swore to curse him and his seed forever. Never quite got that done, though. I wanted to, but somehow, it just never happened. Still. What is written is written and cannot be easily undone. It's a record of a journey, whatever that journey was.

Reuben left then, and moved to a faraway land. He and Ellen were wild and free and together for less than a year. Anyone with half a brain could have known their "love" couldn't last. I certainly could have told them both that. I guess they had to find out on their own. After some years had passed, he moved back into the area to reconnect with his broken family. Mostly with his children, his sons and daughters. He wanted to get back into the daily operations of his business, too. And he reached out to me to see if some kind of reconciliation could be possible. I was extremely skittish when he approached me and put out the feelers. But I didn't discount it. And over time, we got to where we could talk, face to face. And there was a glimmer of what once was before. I could see it was worth repairing, the broken pieces. Time had moved on. It couldn't be what it was before, I figured. The friendship, I mean. But it could be something. Something worth building back up.

And yeah, I was quite aware that there were many people out there who looked at me very strangely as the reconciliation solidified. "What are you thinking? We're lined up here behind you with our swords drawn. Ready to follow and strike and condemn Reuben for all his sins. What's wrong with you? You were real mad. Seething mad, bent to destroy all he is or ever was. And then, all of a sudden, you just laid down your sword. Are you weak or what? How can we hold up our swords when you won't hold up your own? How can we follow when you won't lead?"

And yeah, I heard all that talk. Well, not so much talk as murmurs. I felt those people looking askance all around me. And I felt like telling them, "I am where I am. I choose to walk where I walk. If you think that's weak, that's OK." But my response to all such bloodthirsty Christians would better have been something like this: "Thank you. I appreciate your loyal support. But I got a simple thing to ask. Why don't you live your own lives and let me live mine? What possible business is it of yours what choices I make about who I hang out with?"

And over time, we relaxed a bit, Reuben and me. There was still some tension there, depending on what might come up or what might be triggered in my mind. There were a whole lot of moments like that in my head. But we worked hard at it, he and I, to reach a new dawn. And I have to say, it was all pretty seamless when he returned to the daily operations of his building-supply business, where I am employed.

It was tough for him, outside of my own issues. And no, this is not a sob story about the poor guy. We all pretty much deserve what comes at us, that way. But still, it was tough. There came a whole heck of a lot of judgment out there at him. Totally deserved, I'm sure. But still. At what point does one begin to lower the walls a bit? Even for such a wicked sinner as he was?

There's always a light that comes shining through in a story such as this. Or the telling of it probably wouldn't be happening. And that light came the following November. Reuben and I had taken to hanging out after work every couple of weeks or so. We sipped scotch and talked. (When we reconnected, I swore I would never drink with him. It took more than a year for that little oath to fall by the wayside.) And it was mostly good, always.

One day after work, he seemed a little excited. He had read some article on some website, written by some progressive woman who worked for Fox News. I don't remember her name, and it doesn't matter. But she was pretty well known. She came from the highbrow crowd. She was way too smart, way too educated to believe in such a thing as God. Faith was for hicks. And she wrote about how she came to know Christ. She lived in New York City. The center of the world. And somehow, she was drawn to attend a church there. Redeemer Presbyterian. She heard the sermons of Pastor Tim Keller. And eventually, she wrote, the hound of heaven hunted her down. Jesus stood by her bed in a dream. And asked her to come to Him. And now she knew. Now she believed in Jesus. And she wrote very unashamedly of her journey, of where she was right then and how she got there.

Reuben was fascinated by that article. It was so open and so honest, especially coming from a mainstream media personality. And he followed the link the woman posted to Redeemer Presbyterian. And in less than a week, I saw the change in him. He was listening to those sermons. He told me about it. I had never seen the man more excited. He sent me a link or two. And one Sunday, when I couldn't make it to Chestnut Church, I pulled up that link and listened. Tim Keller is a very dynamic speaker. And no, I don't mean he yells and carries on. He doesn't. He talks very calmly, infusing his message with little stabs of humor. But it's always, always grounded in Scripture. And his message was inside out, from all I ever heard, growing up. Not that I hadn't heard it before. It was right along the same veins that Pastor Mark Potter had been preaching at Chestnut Church for the past number of years. The same stuff. Powerful stuff. Life-changing stuff. It doesn't take you long to grasp the real truth, what real freedom is, when you hear Pastor Mark. And it doesn't take you long when you hear Tim Keller.

Reuben listened and listened to those Tim Keller sermons. I know that because the man wouldn't stop talking about what he was hearing. Always, in every conversation, it got woven in somehow, what he'd heard. And it changed him, too. His personality. He had always been a driven man, as you'd have to be to build up a business like he did. And he had a tendency, sometimes, to let the pressures get to him. He'd get all snappy and uptight and loud. That part of him disappeared almost completely and very soon.

And he told me early on, "Every morning when I get up, that's the first thing I do. I drink coffee and listen to a sermon." Well, what do you do with that? You cheer the man on, in this case. As I did. I was hearing the same stuff at my church, just at more of an entry level. It's preached for people like me, people who come from a guilt-ridden background like the Amish. Here is the path. It's upside down, from all you ever heard. That's what Pastor Mark preached. So I could connect with what Reuben was telling me about what he was hearing.

I thought the whole thing might fade for Reuben. He was living pretty loosely in some areas of his life back in that time. Just like I had lived pretty loosely with my scotch for a long time. And I saw him ponder and reflect on what was and wasn't right. Not as a lost person. But as a child of God, awaking to the light, struggling to grasp, to see, to accept the gift that was there for him. And the next thing I knew, he was driving to New York City every Sunday morning to actually attend services at Redeemer Presbyterian. Right into the big old evil city he went. Week after week, and Sunday after Sunday. And he wouldn't stop talking about what he was hearing. The gospel.

And no, it didn't happen as you'd expect it to in any feel-good Christian story. Where everything suddenly gets all cleaned up and everyone is reunited and singing happy praises. And now everything is perfect. It didn't and it's not. Life is messy, and it's just as messy for Christians as it is for anyone else. At least it is if you're honest. Which a lot of Christians aren't, because they think they have to act all happy and bubbly all the time about what Jesus did for them. That kind of pressure is an awful thing. So this little story doesn't end like that. Reuben did not return to his wife. They are divorced. They remain divorced. I don't judge that. How can I? I'm divorced, too.

And time passed on. A few months later, he told me that

he'd love to start a men's group of some kind. A Bible study, although he didn't call it that. He had in mind that a few guys could just hang out upstairs in the conference room at work. And listen to a Keller sermon. They're only forty minutes long. And then there would be discussion. "Sure," I said. "If that's what your heart's leading you to do, then just do it."

"Ah, I don't know," he said. "I'm not sure anyone will come if I invite them." I told him to try. And he texted a few friends a few weeks after that: "Next Tuesday evening at six thirty. I'd love to see you here for a little get-together. We'll listen to a sermon."

"I'd come," I told him when he asked, "but this week is full. I don't go out evenings much. But go ahead." And that Tuesday, I asked him, "Anyone committed to coming yet?"

"No," he said. "I guess I'll just go and wait and see if anyone shows up." And that was what he did.

The next morning, I asked him, "Well, who came?"

"I had a very nice time," he said bravely. "All by myself." I felt bad for the man. Here he was, all excited. Wanting to just get together with a few guys and share what he had found. And no one came.

"Have one again next Tuesday night," I said. "I'll come if no one else will." And he scheduled the next meeting for the next Tuesday. As that day came, I asked him, "Did anyone commit to come?"

"No," he said. "Are you still coming?"

"I plan to," I said. And I got to thinking. Who could I invite? This was Lancaster County. Everyone was busy all the time. It was tough to get something like this going. I called one friend. He'd like to, but he had other things planned. "That's totally OK," I said. "I just thought I'd check."

Then I thought of another friend, Allen Beiler. He and his family had been coming to my church for some time. I knew he was a market guy, a vendor. Late in the week never suited him. He was at market. But this was Tuesday. So I texted him. "Would you like to come to a Bible study here at the office tonight?" I figured he would have something going.

But he texted right back. "This is a little weird. I was just going to text you to see if you want to go hang out at Vinola's tonight. So, sure, I'll plan on being there."

Great. There will be at least three guys, I thought. *That's better than one, and it's better than two.* I texted Reuben. "My friend Allen's coming. He was going to text me to see if I want to hang out at Vinola's. He's coming here instead."

I just puttered around at my desk after the others left at five. And right at six, Reuben walked in. He had brought snacks and bottled water. He trundled everything upstairs and set it out. Way too much food. And we sat there, talking, the two of us. We kept glancing out toward the road. A few minutes after six thirty, Allen's big old dually pulled in. He parked and walked up to join us. I made the introductions, and we sat and visited for a while. And then Reuben pulled up the sermon he had in mind for that first night.

We sat around the table and listened and took a few

notes. Keller's theme. Is God love or is He judgment? One side claims He's all love. The other side focuses pretty much on judgment. And Keller asked, Does God judge us? Oh, yes, He does. He judges every single thought, every single action, every second of every day. Not that He's standing there with a big old sledgehammer to whack you with if you make a mistake (my words, not his). But He definitely judges everyone, all the time. Keller gets a lot said in forty minutes. He had several closing points. The one I remember was this: if God is the judge, that means we have no right to be. Not saying you don't judge people's actions—this is me speaking again, not Keller. We have to. In business, for instance. If you've given me a bunch of bad checks in the past, I'll insist that you pay cash for any materials you buy from me. Things like that. There are ten thousand more examples.

But we never, never have any right to judge another person's heart. Never. That's God's job. We have no right to be resentful or unforgiving of anyone who's wronged us, either. No matter how deep that wrong was. And yeah, I know a little bit about all that. It takes time, often, to get over a wrong, to heal from a wound that sliced deep. Lots of time, sometimes. And it takes light that can come from only one source. Time. And light. I guess it can all be broken down into two other things Keller kept talking about, too. Forgiveness. And love.

And those two terms don't mean anything close to what I was brought up thinking they mean. Forgiveness isn't so much consciously forgiving someone else for the wrong they did me. It's more like trying to get some small, small

147

grasp of how deeply depraved my own heart is (yes, is—not was) and how much I have been forgiven, simply as a gift, by grace. And love? That's simply loving God.

After the sermon was over, we sat around and talked. And it was open and honest talk. Good stuff, spoken from our hearts. And no, there was no closing prayer, although there certainly would have been nothing wrong with one. We just didn't think about it. By soon after eight or so, we were fixing to leave. And we talked about it. This was great. When can we do it again? We checked our schedules. We settled on the following Tuesday evening. Right there at my office at six thirty p.m. Allen agreed to pick the sermon we'd listen to. Let's try to get a few more people over, we agreed.

And with that, for the first time in my life, I could say I was excited about going to a Bible study. And we put the word out. The invite. If you're a guy, you're welcome to attend, too. We don't care who you are or what you believe. You can be someone who sees things just like we do or close to it. Or you don't have to believe anything about whether or not there is a God. You can be an agnostic or an atheist. You're still welcome. And we're not just saying that. You really are. Yeah, you'll have to listen to a sermon. That might be a negative thing to you. But it's only forty minutes long, and I think you'll be intrigued. And no, you won't get clobbered or ganged up on. You will be totally accepted.

That's the message we wanted to put out. We came up with a couple of rules, and I mean only two. Every person who came was expected to be cordial in speech and conduct, of course. That's always a given. But the only two real rules were this: No drinking at the Bible study. (You could go to the bar afterward, if you wanted to. But you couldn't drink there.) And if you smoked, you had to step outside to do so. It doesn't get much more open than that.

And that's the story of me and Reuben.

MOM'S FUNERAL

THE SPRING OF 2014 came bumping in a little rough. Winter had faded, and new life was sprouting from the earth. Mom had been way under the past few years with that cruel and brutal curse that is Alzheimer's. She hadn't been here, with us. Not in any sense, except for the occasional twinge of coherence. She was out of it in every way. Except her body clung to life. Stayed and lived and breathed. Her condition deteriorated to where we thought she couldn't get any lower, that it couldn't be very long until she got called home. It didn't happen, though. Through it all, she still held on. Held on to life and to this earth. It was a brutal thing to watch.

And it's kind of funny, too, I'm thinking. Writing about traveling home to a funeral while writing about traveling home to another funeral. I think of the prophet Ezekiel in the Old Testament, proclaiming a certain vision he had. Many believe the man saw a spaceship. He described it as a wheel within a wheel, floating up there in the heavens.

Here, it's a funeral within a funeral. Well, the connection makes sense to me. But anyway, back to Mom.

She had been real sick, too, now and then. Not talking about the Alzheimer's, here. She was sick with that, all the way through. That was her condition, her burden, the Alzheimer's. I'm talking sick as in having a fever or some such thing. She was there, so often. And every time that happened, the news trickled out to the family. And every time that happened, we grasped for some small sense of hope. Hope that she could go now. And we prayed that she would be released from all the pain, all the suffering that she could never tell us. We could see it, the state she was in. But she had no voice to tell us. So we simply prayed. That's what you're supposed to do, that's what the preachers tell you. *Lord, take her this time. She has nothing left here.* And we prayed that prayer without guilt.

And we prayed and prayed and prayed some more, those last few years. Prayed that she could go home, that she would be released from her misery, the dark night she was in. All to no avail, it seemed like, as the months came and slipped on by, then the years. And it got to where I despaired of even asking God to take her. It seemed so futile to pray and so utterly senseless that she remained. It just seemed useless to believe that God even heard anything we asked of Him when it came to Mom. To me it did, I mean.

I heard it through all the noise around me. I had just come through another tough March. And now Mom was sick again. It sounded serious this time. *Sure,* I thought. *It's been serious every time.* But this time, it might be different. This time, she had the flu. A serious flu. High fever. And she couldn't cough. She had no strength to. That was where Mom was. That's a pretty cruel place to be. *Lord, take her soon. Take her now.*

And we stayed connected, the family, as that week closed in around us. They were busy, my sister Rosemary and the others in the community. It is a huge burden to take care of someone in Mom's condition at home. It's a constant struggle, a tough road. Get her up. Put her back in bed. Feed her. Get her up again for a few hours. And on and on, over and over. Day after day, week after week. And as time rolled on, year after year.

And every day, we heard the updates on the family chat line. Every day that week, the message was the same. She's sinking. But still, she's hanging on. Thursday and Friday rolled around. She's still sinking. She hasn't been able to take in any food or water since Wednesday. She probably won't last the night. It was an extremely tense and troubled time, that week. Your emotions get yanked around, all over the place. Today her fever is better. And today it's worse again. In the state she was in, no food or water. *God, just take her.* That was the prayer of all her children. And still she hung on. Her heart beat strong.

By Friday, the end seemed imminent. This time, she would go. Very soon. That night, probably. My brother Stephen called me. He and Wilma were heading out that afternoon. They'd arrive tomorrow, on Saturday. I wished him a safe trip. And told him I'd come when something happened. "Those are decisions we all have to make for ourselves," I said. "By all means, go. Give my greetings to the others. Tell them I hope to see them soon."

You only get one mother. And there are all kinds of emotions involved in letting her go when death comes calling. She can leave only once. But in a sense, Mom had already left us long ago. First into the twilight, then into the sheer and brutal darkness that is Alzheimer's. What do you do when those opposing emotions collide? You want her to be released from all that pain and crap she's going through. But your heart doesn't want to release the woman who gave birth to you, the woman who brought you into this life.

That week, as she sank lower and lower, my emotions bounced all over. But the strongest one was a deep longing to see her released from this earth. Maybe I'm a bad son. I don't know. But that's what I felt, and I would bet that's what all my siblings felt, too. It was just so frustrating as each day came and went. *Lord, please call her home to You. Please.* And yet He wouldn't. Day after day after day, as she sank into a weaker and weaker place, her heart still beat, strong as ever. It was all pretty maddening.

Saturday crept by, then Sunday came. And that morning, in church, I talked to my pastor, Mark Potter. Told him of Mom's condition. How she was clinging on. And how we were praying for her release. Mark jotted down a few notes and included my prayer to open the sermon that morning. He spoke Mom's name. "Ira's mother, Ida Mae." Her age. Her condition. He prayed for her peaceful passing.

And I told my friends at church how it was. They'd all known. "Still, we think it's getting close," I said. "We just don't know. Pray that she'll leave us soon." And all that day, no news. That night, I sat at my computer, writing. And right out of nowhere, all at once, I just got real mad.

Pastor Mark had always preached, "God is your Father. A father wants to hear what's in your heart. If you're not happy about something, if you're angry about something that's going on in your life, just tell Him. He wants to hear it. Tell Him." And that night, sitting here, I did just that.

I was pretty mad. And I let Him know that. I told Him. "You are God. Why in the world are you keeping this poor woman here? She's suffering, just as she's been for years. What purpose can you possibly have to let her linger and waste away like that? Come on. You can call her home anytime you're of a mind to. Call her to you. Now. Tonight. Why, why wouldn't you do that? It's such a simple thing. Call her home. Take her to you. All it takes is one word from you, one breath of your command. Call her home. Now."

I slept fitfully that night. The next morning, I got up. It was Monday, April 28, 2014. I immediately checked the messages. No news. Mom was still with us. I got ready and drove to work. And I remembered my talk with God the night before. And I remember exactly where I was driving when I muttered to God that morning on the road, "Yeah, I'm still mad. You can take her home. Why don't you? Just do it. Right now."

And it turned out that pretty much right that moment, when I was muttering to God to hear me, He did.

I got to work and parked. Walked in. We were short-handed that morning. Only two other office workers and me. And they both asked, "Any news about your mom?"

"Nope," I said. "She's real bad and sinking. But her heart

is strong. She's still here with us." And just about then, a few minutes before seven, I heard the ping. A text. I'd been jumpy about those for days. I pulled out my iPhone. And there it was on the screen. A message from my brother Stephen: "Mom died at 6:42 a.m."

That was it. And I felt it rushing through me, a huge wave of relief, mixed with a whole lot of other emotions. "She's gone," I half shouted to the others. "Mom is gone. She just died a few minutes ago. At 6:42."

What can you possibly remember about a moment like that? Or try to write? But I focused in. The next thing I needed to know was when the funeral would be. They had told us, the Aylmer people, that there was a wedding on Thursday. Weddings take precedence over funerals, as they should. So depending on when Mom passed, the funeral would be on Wednesday or on Friday. And it was getting real tight on a Monday morning to have it on Wednesday. I texted Stephen back. "When is the funeral?" And then I sat at my desk and tried to focus on my work. That was impossible, of course.

And my cell phone started ringing, right along. My sister Rachel called. And Magdalena. I'm not sure who all else. They got it decided pretty quick, up there in Aylmer. The funeral would be on Wednesday. The day after tomorrow. That wasn't much time to get up there. By three, I was on the road. My rented Charger pulsed along silently. And my phone kept ringing as I was driving. My niece Janice called. She wasn't going to get into Buffalo until eleven. And I mentioned to her that I figured to get a room at her motel. "Oh," she said. "I have a lot of points saved up. Let me see if I can get you a room." And she called back a bit later. She had booked a room for me at the Courtyard by Marriott right by the airport. The place where she was staying. "Just walk in and tell them your name," she told me. "They'll have a room for you."

I thanked her. "We'll connect tomorrow morning," I said.

And right around eight thirty p.m., just as my GPS had claimed, I pulled into the Courtyard by Marriott parking lot. Just a little over five and a half hours from home, that's how far Buffalo is from me. It was a very fancy place, the hotel. Large and new and gleaming. The nice lady checked me in, camo jacket and all. I almost hadn't brought a jacket with me. It was warm back home. But at the last minute, I took the light camo jacket from my truck and threw it in the rental. It was the only coat of any kind I took. And I would come to regret that, big time.

I settled in my room, then walked down to the little Bistro in the lobby. Sat at the bar and ordered a sandwich and a scotch. Janice had texted earlier. Her flight was delayed again. She wouldn't be in until close to midnight. After relaxing with my food and drink, I walked back to my room. Tomorrow would be a different kind of day. A very different kind of day.

There had never been a death of any kind in my immediate family. Never. Dad and Mom had eleven children. From nine of those children came fifty-nine grandchildren and ninety-eight great-grandchildren, as of 2014. And out of all those people, none had died. My family had never had any funeral of any kind, not to where the others would come. Sure, I think there were four stillbirths along the way. But those don't really count, because those stillborn children never lived or breathed. And that's pretty astounding, any way you look at it. All those children, all those grandchildren, and all those great-grandchildren. And no funerals for any of them. It had to be some sort of record, I thought to myself. Or close to one.

And now a funeral was coming. As funerals should come. Children burying a parent. Not the other way around. It had come close to being the other way around, though. My brother Titus comes to mind, with his accident back in 1982. He almost died. He would have after another twenty or thirty seconds under the water. And he was wounded, very much so. But he didn't die. My brother Joseph got real sick, too. He had almost died a few months before, from pneumonia. And I was just coming out of my own heart problems right around the time Mom passed. I could have died. But none of us did. We all hung on. There never was a funeral before Mom's, not in my immediate family. Not a funeral for a real live person who had lived and breathed. That was all coming up real soon, though. Those were the thoughts I had that night at the Courtyard.

Janice got in real late. And I went to sleep before she ever arrived. The next morning, we met down at the Bistro. She was groggy and a bit hungry. I ate some yogurt. She ordered French toast and gave me a slice. And then we were off in the Charger. I had to gas up first before we got into Canada. They charge crazy prices up there for petrol. I told Janice, "I can fill up here, and it'll be enough to get us there and back."

We filled up at a station. And then it was off to the

border. The rain started coming down, hard. The Charger took it all in stride, though. There's no better car to drive through the rain than a Charger. And soon enough, we arrived at the border. A glum guard took our passports. "What are you doing in Canada?" she asked.

"Going to my mom's funeral," I said. She made no noises of condolence at all. Just handed back our passports and waved us through. And then we were off, into the rain.

And we pushed our way along, in and out through the traffic, and on and on and on and on. And soon, Aylmer loomed. Our destination. The place where Mom was. I was calm as we approached the area. The flat earth. The little groves of trees, scattered here and there on the land. "This is the area where I grew up," I told Janice. "This is the land I knew as a child."

We drove along, straight south. Aylmer was coming right up. And then we arrived. And headed right on west to Saint Thomas and our motel. The rain subsided. Saint Thomas finally was before us. And the Comfort Inn, where everyone was staying. We pulled in and parked. Other vehicles from all over sat parked. We met some of my nieces and nephews from various places, all milling about, getting ready to head out to the farm where Mom was.

Thirty minutes later, Janice and I had changed into funeral clothes and were ready. I felt it stirring inside, the moment that was coming. Yeah, I had felt mostly relief when Mom passed. Huge relief that she'd suffer no more on this earth. But now, now I was actually heading out to see her. It just felt very strange. "This is a new place for me," I told Janice.

"It's a new place for all of us," she said.

We arrived at Joe and Rosemary Gascho's farm, where my parents had lived in their little *Daudy* house for the past few years. We parked over to the south of the house in a little lot set off for cars. Everything was muddy, everywhere, from the rain. And now the wind was blowing hard. Lester, Rosemary's son who had taken over the home farm, met us outside. We followed him across the planks laid down over the muddy yard and garden, up to the old redbrick farmhouse.

It was probably one thirty or so in the afternoon. They had eaten at noon but saved some food for us. "We'll go in first, to see Mom, then we'll come back to eat," I told the cooks. They smiled patiently. And Janice and I walked up the steps from the washhouse into the kitchen. There weren't many people around right at that moment. Mostly my siblings, and a few neighbors and friends. Dad was nowhere to be seen. He was upstairs, taking a nap, they told us. My sisters and my brothers Jesse and Stephen came to greet us. We all hugged each other unashamedly.

They all looked exhausted. But Rosemary smiled in welcome. "We'll take you in to see Mom," she said. And they led us into the little bedroom in the northwest corner of the house. A small room, really. It had been Rosemary and Joe's bedroom for decades. We walked through the door. The coffin was set up in the middle of the room. There was no furniture except for a dresser on the far north side by the wall. On that dresser sat a small mantel clock. Stopped at 6:42 a.m. The moment Mom had died.

I approached the coffin, Janice beside me. The others

stood around close. And there she lay. Mom. Small, shrunken, impossibly frail, in a new black dress and a new large white head covering. Lying there in the white-lined coffin, her head resting on a small new pillow. I stood there, beside the coffin, and just looked at her. Here was Mom. Here was death. So real and so final. It was here, in this room. Janice stood close, her arm around me. I felt it all deep down inside, and the tears trickled out. My sisters wept with me. Mom. Right here. Gone. She would never suffer on this earth again. But still. She was gone.

And I whispered to Janice, "Is it OK if I touch her face?"

"Yes, yes," she whispered back. "It's all right." I reached down and gently stroked her cold and leathered cheeks. Mom.

And my sisters and brothers told me of how it was, the details of Mom's journey in those final days. How she had passed peacefully in that last hour. They had been there when she died. Staying up with her. Her hands had gotten real cold in the early morning hours. And they knew it was coming. Jesse said she wouldn't die until the day broke. And she didn't. When the time came, they saw her breath of life giving up. From her chest on up it came. Then through her throat. And then to her mouth. The breath of life expired, right there. That's what they told me.

And there are always the stories, the stories that come. It's such a part of Amish lore and tradition. Always there are stories, the stories of dying. And there, as we stood looking down at Mom, Rosemary and Naomi told me a very special one.

Back the week before, as Mom was sinking, the nurse that came out to check on her told my sisters, "It's important that the family releases your mother. You must tell her it's all right if she goes. Otherwise, she may hang on for longer than she has to."

So on Thursday, Rosemary and Naomi cleared everyone out of her bedroom and closed the door. They stood on each side of her bed and held her hands. And Rosemary spoke to Mom. "We are here, Naomi and me. We want to tell you that it's all right for you to go. If you hear Jesus calling you, go to Him." And she talked some more, about what a good Mom she had been and how she was loved by all her children. And at the end, she told Mom, "Now, if you heard what I said, can you squeeze my hand?" And Mom squeezed the hand that Naomi held. It was her strongest hand, the one that Rosemary held was barely functional anymore. So they figure she heard what Rosemary told her. And understood.

The Amish have stories, and they also have dreams and visions, especially at such a time when death approaches. It's just part of the culture. And Rosemary told me of one such dream. On the Saturday night before Mom passed, the neighbors came around to be with her, too. There was someone at her bedside twenty-four hours a day. And that night, at midnight, Junior and Wilma Eicher came to take their turn. Junior was the son of my childhood preacher, Jake Eicher, and Wilma was Junior's wife. They came to stay from midnight until six in the morning.

Wilma was very tired, so she retired on the bed off to the side of the room. And drifted off into deep slumber.

I don't know how she heard what she heard. But she told the others that she heard beautiful, beautiful singing. Mom's voice, joined by a man's, startlingly clear and utterly beautiful. That was what she claimed she heard. When she stirred a bit later and came out of the dream, she asked her husband, "Were you singing with Mommy? I heard beautiful singing. And there was a strong voice singing with her, from a man."

And Junior told her, "No, I've been awake. There was no singing, not that I heard. She's lying here, just the same as always."

Dreams and visions. Who knows what was really going on? Maybe those were angels singing with Mom. Or maybe it was just a dream from the exhausted mind of an exhausted woman who slept by the deathbed of my mother. They take comfort from such dreams and visions, the Amish do. This time, it was a dream of Mom singing. Of angels singing. And right at that moment, when I heard about it, that dream gave me comfort, too.

We walked back out to the kitchen, then. There were no flowers anywhere. That's one thing you'll never see at any Amish funeral. It's just the way it's always been. It's a somber time, a funeral, and not a time for flowers. A row of chairs was set up in front. A bench along the back wall. Facing all that, just outside and to the right of the bedroom door, there was a comfortable office chair. For Dad. And a single chair beside his. Dad wasn't around right then. He was still upstairs, taking a nap. And soon enough, the word came down from Dorothy, Janice's older sister. They had told Dad, "Ira and Janice just got here." And right away, he wanted to come down. Right away. He wanted to see Janice.

There always was a special bond between Dad and Janice. She was his favorite grandchild, or certainly one of them. It was because she had worked hard over the years to build a good relationship with him. And it could not be denied. She also reminded him a lot of her mother and his daughter, Magdalena. We walked into the living room and opened the stairwell door. Dorothy was helping Dad down the steps. It was a little tricky with his cane. Janice went halfway up to help them both. And I met them at the bottom. He shook our hands and greeted us. Then he walked into the kitchen and sat on his designated chair. Janice sat beside him. And the two of them just talked, oblivious to the clamor of the room.

I had wondered, on the way up to Aylmer, *Sure, my clan will come in force. But will the others come? Mom was just a few months shy of her ninety-first birthday when she died. How important will it be to the other families? Dad's nieces and nephews. They're scattered all over creation. How important will it be to some of them to come?* And that afternoon, there wasn't a whole lot going on. Not a lot of people around, except immediate family. And it seemed right then like there wouldn't be that large a crowd showing up.

After visiting with Dad for half an hour or so, Janice got up. I went and sat on the chair beside Dad. He looked old and very tired. The man was almost beside himself with grief. But he was there, with it. He fully grasped what had happened. And he told me little snippets of his memories of Mom. How she was always so helpful and kind to everyone. And how she worked so hard. "She didn't have a slow speed. When she walked, she almost ran," he said. His voice was slow and very heavy. He was alone now, all alone. And the realization of all of that was pressing in on him hard.

Janice and a group of my other nephews and nieces headed back to the motel to rest up a bit for the evening. I wanted to go along. I was beyond tired, almost exhausted. But I figured I'd better stay with the family. *This is Mom's funeral. You have to stay and absorb all you can.* We sat there, and people trickled through. By late afternoon, Titus and Ruth arrived with their boys. We got Titus inside with the portable ramps he had brought along for wheelchair access to the house. We got him comfortable in the kitchen. We all went with him into the room where Mom was, and my sisters told him the stories they had told me. Dad came in, too. He stood there forlornly beside the coffin. He suddenly reached down and covered Mom's folded hands with his own.

Supper was served at five, and the grandchildren came back for that. After we ate, the siblings lined up, pretty much by age, on the chairs and benches in the kitchen. And all at once, it just seemed like the floodgates opened. People began arriving from all over. Strangers, total strangers, at least to me, from the nearby Amish communities of Lakeside and Mount Elgin. Plainer places. These people came because they knew and remembered Mom. And the relatives poured in, too. Uncle Abner Wagler's children came—the locals and some from far away. Yeah, the clans would make it. I needn't have fretted about that. As the people filed through and shook our hands, I thanked each one for taking the time and making the effort. "Oh, we wouldn't have missed it," they said.

Dad's younger sister Rachel Graber got there early that evening. They had traveled from Kalona, Iowa. (Every living member of Rachel's family made it to the funeral. That was a huge honor to my family.) Rachel hobbled up to Dad with her cane. He didn't see her until she was close. And he struggled to his feet to greet her. The two of them were all that remained of all their immediate family. Everyone else had moved on. And they stood there and just talked. I could not hear the conversation—too much noise and too many people. I saw Dad leading Aunt Rachel into the bedroom where Mom was. My sisters followed, and they shut the door. The memories flooded in for Aunt Rachel, too. They had even shared their wedding day, she and Mom. A double wedding. And she just stood there, bent over her cane, and looked down on Mom with gentle grief as the memories swept through her.

People just kept coming and coming. Rosemary and her family had removed every stick of furniture from the bottom floor of the old redbrick house. And set up rows and rows of benches in every room. After visitors had filed through the bedroom where Mom was, they filed past us, Dad and the children. And then into the back rooms, where they were seated on the benches. A steady hum of voices buzzed through the house. Two van loads of people arrived from Daviess County, Indiana. Mom's younger sister Annie's children and a dozen or so Amish relatives, cousins and nephews and nieces and such. There is something pretty distinct about the Daviess people. Their dress and their features. You can tell if someone comes from Daviess. I thanked each one as they filed past us. Thanks for coming. Thanks for honoring my mother.

Rosemary had told me. At seven thirty p.m., the youth would come and sing. They arrived. There was no room for them in the house, so they lined up, standing in the attached washhouse. The door between was open. And right on cue, they began. It was chillingly, chillingly beautiful. And everything got all quiet in the house as everyone just sat and listened. A few German songs first. Then a few English ones. All about heaven and leaving this vale of tears for that beautiful place. "Dad picked out those songs," my sister Rachel whispered to me. "Well, someone may have helped him."

And as the singing soared around us, I turned to Nathan, who was sitting beside me. Whispered, "Do you want to go in to see Mom with me?" He nodded immediately. So the two of us got up, filed around, and walked into the bedroom. I shut the door behind us.

It was all so surreal, hearing those singing voices fading in and out, and being there in that bedroom with Nathan and Mom. The door opened then, and Jesse stepped in to join us. We just stood around the coffin, and I reached down and stroked her face. Her poor frail body had seen and suffered so much. She looked peaceful, though, lying there. The undertaker had done a real good job, the family told me. He had made her sunken face and cheeks stand out almost like normal. Jesse left us then, and Nathan and I just stood in silence beside our mother for a few more minutes. Then I propped the door open, and we walked back to our seats.

Just before nine, the crowd was dismissed. A preacher I didn't know got up and stood at an open doorway between two rooms. Spoke in a loud, firm voice. Everyone got real quiet. And he spoke for a few minutes, giving a short devotional and sharing a few memories of Mom. The Amish don't focus on the name of the deceased. Or much of what they ever did while here. False praise, they call that. But still, a little of that is OK. This preacher spoke of death and how it must come for us all. The important thing is to be ready. Then he asked us all to stand as he read a High German prayer from a little black prayer book.

The next morning, I dressed in my white shirt and black suit and shoes. The funeral would start at nine. There was a private service at seven thirty a.m. at the house. I arrived just as it was about to start. The coffin had been moved into the living room. A few benches were lined up in front. Mostly for my dad and siblings, although anyone from the extended family was welcome. We sat there as my cousin Simon Wagler, Abner's son and a preacher, stood to speak. He still sounded the same as he had when I was a child. A good voice that carried well. And he, too, made mention that at Amish funerals, they don't falsely praise the departed. But he had many memories of Aunt Ida Mae, and he shared a few. About how she was always so cheerful, always smiling, and always hard at work. Some brief admonitions followed, then we knelt for prayer, again read from that little black prayer book.

And after that, the pallbearers came and closed the lid.

And they carried Mom from the house. The funeral would be about half a mile north. In a huge shop where gazebos were manufactured. Everything had been cleared out, and countless rows of benches had been set up. I arrived around eight thirty or so, along with most of my siblings. They had a special section for all of us, right up front by the coffin. We settled in by age, all my siblings and their partners and I. Aunt Rachel was given a seat of high honor among us. The place filled up to the brim. Hundreds and hundreds of people. All filed in silently, all were directed to their seats. All had come to honor Mom.

There is no singing at an Amish funeral. Just two or three fairly short sermons and a prayer. A few minutes before nine, local bishop John Martin stood. And the service began. The funeral service for Mom. John preached hard and sat down right on time. Then another bishop stood. Tim Coblentz, from Mays Lick, Kentucky. My parents had lived there, in his community, for a few years with my brother Joseph. So Tim knew them. The poor man had a bit of a cold but somehow made it through.

By ten fifteen a.m., the preaching was done. We knelt for a long prayer, and then were seated again. And they began filing past the coffin, all the assembled masses. It takes a good bit of time for six hundred people to get through. That's how many they told me were there, later. Six hundred. That's a pretty huge crowd. And finally it reached my family section. They filed through, all the grandchildren, many with children of their own. Slowly, some lingering to look at the woman they have always known as "Mommy." And then it came to us, the children.

From the oldest down, we went. One by one, and we each had a brief moment alone with her. I reached down and stroked her tired face one more time. And then we were seated. And Dad struggled to his feet, and hobbled slowly to where his wife lay, waiting for him.

He stood there, half bent, over her. He looked so tired and so alone. He reached down and covered her small hands with one of his. And then the children, just the children, got up and went up front to join him.

It's always a deeply moving and touching thing, the family surrounding the coffin of a departed one. We stood there, huddled around, and wept with our father. It was the first time since 1971 that all of us were together, that close to each other like that. It's just how it happened back then. A few of the older ones left the Amish. And somehow, it never worked out in forty-three years that all of us were together at the same place at the same time. That's a long, long time, and it's a real shame. But it is what it is. We were all together there, around my mother's coffin. And after a few intense minutes, we turned and walked back to our seats. And soon the service was dismissed.

The pallbearers loaded the casket into the hearse then. Well, it was a buggy. Specially built. To function as an everyday buggy. But also to function as a hearse. And the train of buggies lined up behind. We wouldn't join that line, those of us with cars. No. This day, we respected the place, the community that cared for Mom all these years. The Aylmer community. We puttered about, those of us in cars. And then we headed over on the main drag through the community. A different route than the buggies were taking. And we pulled right onto the gravel road leading to the graveyard. Plenty of cars and vans were already parked. I parked in line. And we got out and walked to join the crowd.

The grave had been dug the day before, right in the driving rain. But it had been covered up with plywood. That old Daviess adage still holds in Aylmer, I think. Don't ever let it rain into an open grave. If you do, someone else in the community will die within three weeks. They hadn't let the rain in. And today, the day of the funeral, there was a canopy set up. Right over the grave. I can't imagine that such a thing had ever been done before in Aylmer. But today, they did it. For Mom.

We gathered under the canopy, the family members who had gotten there in cars. Waiting for Mom to arrive in the buggy. The pallbearers stood around. And I approached them and talked to them. "The sons would like to help fill the grave," I said. It wasn't a request. I was just telling them.

And they told me, "That will be no problem. Just wait a bit after the coffin is lowered. We get down, two of us, on the wooden lid. And we fill all that dirt in by hand." They do that in Aylmer. I'm not sure if that's a universal thing or a remnant of a tradition from Daviess. But they step down, right on the lid of the box enclosing the coffin. And the other two pallbearers hand down the dirt, shovelful after shovelful. The two standing on the box fill in the edges. And then the top. It's all done carefully. "Wait," they told me, the pallbearers. "Wait until we step up out of the grave. Then we'll hand the shovels to you and your brothers."

And I passed the word around to the family. My brothers and I will step up and help shovel the dirt in. If any of you nephews want to step up, too, get in line. This is Mom. We need to get involved, to cover her up.

The buggy train arrived soon. And parked off in the little lot out on the south side of the graveyard. The hearse pulled right in. And the pallbearers unloaded Mom and set up the casket on the west end of the grave. Opened it up for the last time. There would be one more viewing. Sometimes it seems like they almost overdo things, the Amish. We'd all viewed her back at the service. And now we'd all view her again. They lifted back the coffin lid. And there she lay again. Open to all the world for one last time.

This, this is what I'd asked Janice to come for. At my Uncle Abner's funeral, the children had all walked up, one by one, with their families. But strangely, that wasn't how it came down for Mom. The crowds filed by one last time. And then it was time for the family. Janice stood beside me. But we didn't walk up one by one. We walked up in line. We filed through. And then Dad stood there alone and covered Mom's hands with his again one last time. Then he hobbled back to his seat. The Amish funeral director stepped up. Folded down the coffin lid. I craned and caught a last glimpse of Mom's face as the lid closed. He stood there with his screwdriver. And drove in the screws. Then he stepped back. The pallbearers approached and lifted the coffin. They had set two boards across the open grave. They set the coffin on those boards.

Then they set the straps under the coffin. Lifted it a few inches. The director removed the boards set across the hole. And then the pallbearers lowered her into the earth, into the wooden box down at the bottom of the grave. They rolled up their straps. And reset them through the handles on the box lid. Then they lowered the lid. And again retrieved their straps.

Two of them got down into the grave then, just as they had told me they would. The other two handed down shovels full of dirt. The two men standing on the box carefully placed that dirt around the edges. And then they carefully placed dirt above the lid they were standing on. It was a somber and respectful thing. Minutes passed, and still they were handing down shovels full of dirt. And placing it carefully where it needed to go.

Then the moment came. The lid was covered. The two men in the grave scrambled out. This was our time now, our time, my family's. I whispered to Stephen, who was standing right beside me, "It's time to step up."

He whispered back, "Are you sure it's all right?" I didn't answer. Because the man closest to me was turning to me, just like he had said he would. Handing me his shovel. I stepped up. And Stephen stepped up. The pallbearers stepped back. We walked to the other side of the grave. I stabbed my shovel into the mound of soft, sandy dirt. And turned and dropped that dirt onto Mom's new house.

It was purely symbolic, what I had in mind. It wasn't like we had to cover her grave all the way to the top. Just a few shovels thrown, that was all I wanted to do. Steve was off to the left side of the grave. I was on the right side. And after about a dozen throws of dirt, I stopped. Turned back to where the family stood. And motioned to Nathan.

Come. He stepped up, and I handed him the shovel. And right then, Steve handed his shovel off to Jesse. I stood back, among the family. And right before my eyes, the most beautiful thing unfolded, the most beautiful thing that I'll ever remember about my mother's funeral.

They started lining up, and they stepped up, one by one. First, the sons. Then the sons-in-law. A moment only to shovel, for each of them. It could have stopped with us, the immediate family, Mom's children and sons-in-law. But it didn't. All of a sudden, the nephews were lining up. And stepping up to take their turns with the shovels. The men of the family. They came and shoveled the earth onto the grave. And then suddenly four of my sisters stood in line: Magdalena, Naomi, Rachel, and Rhoda.

Such a thing had never happened in Aylmer before. Never. I don't think the sons stepping up had ever happened before. And now here came the daughters. And more nephews and then the nieces. All stepping forward to bury their mother and grandmother. I look back on the whole experience, and this moment was the most precious of all the moments. A purely beautiful thing of respect and love. I almost choke up, thinking about it even from here.

And eventually, the family was done. The last ones handed the shovels back to the pallbearers. And Mom got covered up real quick right after that happened. And then the ceremony was over. I left soon after it ended. Too soon, I think. Because the grandchildren broke out in song right there beside the grave. I missed it, the singing.

And here, I publicly thank the people of Aylmer. It was a vast communal effort just to take care of Mom during her last few years on this earth. Of course, most of that burden fell on my sister Rosemary and her family. It was a hard and wearying thing for them, but they never complained. They just did what they needed to do to show Mom that she was loved. And to make her as comfortable as possible. The people in the community, the people of Aylmer came and helped, too.

And during Mom's final days, they came at night to sit with her. There is a deep aversion in the Amish culture. You don't allow anyone to die alone. It's important that the dying person has people around. And all through the night, every night, they took turns in six-hour shifts. That takes effort, and that takes commitment. They came through, strong and shining, the people of Aylmer. And I thank all of them from the bottom of my heart. All of them. Thank you for caring for my mother. Thank you for loving her, even in that helpless state.

We all gathered back at the big shop for the noon meal. The Aylmer people fed us, a huge horde of people, for two days. I walked through the line, got my food. Ham-and-cheese sandwiches, noodles, mashed potatoes, and potato salad. And I sat way off in one corner by myself to eat. But not for long. Soon, very soon, people wandered by to see me. I was a little startled at such attention.

The first person was an old man, gray and half-stooped. I recognized him. He sat on the next bench over as I ate. "Do you know who I am?" he asked.

"Yes," I said. "I know who you are."

And he spoke half-apologetically. "I'm sorry that you had to carry my name all your life. I'm Ira Stoll. I was working on the farm the day you were born. You were named after me."

I laughed. "Don't apologize," I said. "I used to hate my name. But I don't anymore. Actually, I like it. I'm proud of it. It's pretty unique." And we talked about the things he saw, the world he knew, way back when I was born. It was a special moment.

Nathan and I had one last thing to do on that day as late afternoon approached. We had talked about it and agreed on a plan. And we walked out and got into the Charger. Drove over to Aylmer and stopped by the flower shop at the west side of the square. We walked in. The place smelled just lovely. And we picked out two beautiful red roses. "Do you want anything with these? Baby's breath?" the attendant asked.

Nathan shook his head. "Nothing. Just the roses." She wrapped them in separate plastic sleeves. Nathan paid her and thanked her.

The skies were spitting random drops of rain as we pulled up to the graveyard. The place was empty and deserted, all cleaned up. The canopy was gone. I parked off to the side of the road, and we got out. Nathan handed me my rose. This wouldn't take long. We climbed over the low wooden fence and walked to the grave. We stood side by side in silence for a moment. Then we stooped together and placed the roses on the soft earth above our mother.

Nathan spoke to her. "You were a good mom," he said. "A good mom. You had a hard life. I'm so glad you can finally rest now."

"Yes," I said. "You were a good mom. I'm glad, too, that you are at peace now."

And then I turned to Nathan and told him, "Of all her sons, of all her children, we hurt her the most, you and I. We caused her the most turmoil, the most anguish, the most pain. Of all her sons."

He nodded. "Yes. We did."

We stood there, heads bowed, for a few more seconds. And then we turned and walked back to the road.

Behind us, Mom slept peacefully in her new house, where the cold and bitter winds could never reach her.

A DAY THAT WILL
NEVER COME

YOU LOOK, WHEN something happens, how long it takes to circle around to the other side. When Ellen and I separated in 2007, that was a brutal time. The divorce got finalized later that year, sometime in November. And we never communicated much those first few years. Once in a while, there'd be a strained email about some logistical thing. And when I settled on our house, then we communicated some, too. I got the house appraised, then remortgaged. And I bought out her half of the equity that was there. There weren't a whole lot of pangs in me about all that. Some, sure. It was so final, so irrevocable, seemed like. With every step, the separation just got that much more firm, more deeply poured in concrete. But mostly, it all went well.

And I won't pretend otherwise. The ghosts of who we were lurked there in the old brick house we had shared as our home. I stayed rooted there, because I was too stubborn to get pushed out by the memories of what had been or the hauntings of what might have been. So now and then I wrestled with the ghosts, when they came. "Go away," I told them. "Leave me alone." And mostly, they did. But sometimes they returned with a vengeance, and the battle started all over again. That's just how it was.

The years kind of slide together here in my memory. I can't quite remember the dates of what happened when. Anyway, it wasn't all that long after Ellen moved out west that the word trickled back. She was dating some guy she met there. About my age, the man was. His name was Tim. I brooded a good bit when I heard that. Still, you just keep walking. And I will say, I never, never blamed Tim for anything. He was just a guy who came wandering along long after me and my ex-wife had blown up our marriage. I always figured he was probably a pretty likable man. But still...but still.

And I remember the turmoil inside me when I heard. Ellen and Tim were engaged. They were going to get married in July of 2010, if I remember right. That was the summer I was writing my first book. So there was a lot going on. Still, as the date approached, I brooded a good bit. It wasn't right that I sat here all alone while she went gallivanting around, and now she was getting married again. That's the concept that was so strange. Where we both came from, you just didn't see such a thing. No divorce. And for sure no divorce and remarriage. And the ghosts kept pushing themselves forward into my mind. There she was, way out there. And here I was, back where our future dreams together had been launched, not all that many years ago. I brooded and drank and brooded and wrote. How a book ever came out of me that summer is more than a miracle.

The date approached, her new wedding date, I mean. And as it got close, I had to get out of the house. That Friday, the day before, I boarded my truck and headed west to Daviess, the land of my ancestors. My fatherland. There was a little gathering going on that I figured to attend. Some old historic Amish house in Daviess was going to be torn down soon. And that Saturday, the place was open to all who wanted to walk through it one last time. The house had been in my blood lineage, on my mother's side, I think. Anyway, I just figured I should hit the road and drive. Maybe I could get my head cleared.

It was a real good trip, more than I could ever have hoped for. I connected with the *Freundschaft* that Saturday and hung out with friends and relatives. I thought of the wedding now and then but only fleetingly. *Ellen is getting married this afternoon.* Overall, the trip went better than I had dared to hope it would. And the next morning, early, I headed back east toward home.

I got back late that afternoon. And I walked into my home. And it was one of the strangest things I had ever felt. The ghosts were gone. There was no vestige, no hint of their presence. Whatever had existed between Ellen and me, that time was past now. It was so clear. Now she belonged to another man. Coming from where I came from, this was a very strange place to be. But there I was. And since that day, the ghosts of our pasts, Ellen's and mine, have never returned.

We communicate now in a way I never figured we

would. We can, anyway. We don't that much. But we can and do. A few years after Mom passed away, Ellen's father, Adin, died. We communicated both times. She contacted me before Mom's funeral. And she told me, "Back when we separated, you told me you didn't want to go alone to your mother's funeral. I promised then that I would come and go with you. Do you need me to?" I was touched that she remembered. I thanked her and declined the offer.

And when Adin passed, I called her. And we simply spoke for a few minutes. "I remember how you tried hard, so hard, to reach your dad," I said. "And he never would let you. He always rejected you. I never forgot how that was." And we grieved for a few minutes, at the tragedy of all we had seen together. And we cried a little bit together, too.

In time, then, Ellen and I looked after each other and cared for each other about as much as two people coming from where we came from could have. We emailed briefly now and then about this and that. And I've always said, pretty much, I don't mind talking to Ellen and even seeing her here and there. I would be OK if I randomly ran into her and her husband, Tim. I'd be good with that as long as I wasn't expecting it. But then I always poured a little bit of concrete. I will not deliberately go to a place where I know they both will be. A day like that is a day that will never come.

The summer of 2016. Ellen's brother Paul has a large party every summer in July. It happens out on his large back deck every year. The formal tables are set up. He cooks up a great feast. And all the guests dress up in white. That year, I looked at the invitation. All other years, I was all ambivalent in my response. Maybe I'll make it. Paul and I both knew I had no intention of showing up. That's how it always was before. But not this time.

That year, the invite came in the spring, like it always does. And this time, I looked at it in a way I never had before. *Yes. I will do this. An outdoor party. I can wear my white pants, a white shirt, and my seersucker jacket. And my little white hat. I think that would work out just fine. I will go to places like Paul's White Party.* That's what I thought to myself. Step out. Live a little. And I told Paul, "I'm coming this year, for the first time ever. Looking forward to it."

I think he was a little surprised. But he didn't let on. "Great," he said. And that's how we left it early on. But then, a few weeks later, he had something more to tell me.

I don't remember if he called me or just sent me a text message. It's not that important, either way. But somehow, he told me, "Ellen wants to come for the White Party this year. She and Tim are going to be here. Are you OK with that?"

And right there it was. The day I had told myself would never come. I would not walk deliberately into a place where I knew my ex-wife and her husband would be. It wasn't something I got showed how to do, growing up. It was always the outside English people who got caught up in traps like that. And I remember hearing of such a thing here and there, and wondering how it could be. *How can any former husband and wife be at the same place in peace, especially when a new spouse is right there, too?* I've always wondered. And I've always thought, *That's for those people to figure out. It's not me.*

But now it was me.

I wrote back and told Paul that I planned to be there. And that's how we left it. The date slowly drifted in and came at us.

The party was in late July. And as the day approached, I got to thinking it might be real hot that evening, too hot for a suit coat. And then the week arrived. And was it ever hot all week. The sun scorched down every day, and the hottest temps of the week were forecast for Saturday afternoon. And then the day arrived.

It felt so strange, walking up to a new door like that. I felt no stress at all, and no flashbacks came at me all week. The actual morning dawned, and the day crept by. And by four I was dressed and ready. White pants, seersucker shirt, white hat. And I cruised up north on the forty-five minute drive to Paul's big mansion.

I pulled in right at five and parked. I was a good bit early. I had planned it that way. I couldn't stay late, because of some other things going on. So I figured I'd get there early and get some visiting done. I walked into the garage, where Paul greeted me. "I'm early," I said.

"That's totally all right," he said. I turned toward the house. And she came walking through the foyer and out into the garage. She was smiling.

It was Ellen. The woman I had married almost precisely sixteen years before that moment. It had been a good number of years since it had all blown up, and we had both aged a bit. I'd aged the most, of course. I was old and gray haired now. Gray bearded, too. But she was still as beautiful as ever. Her smile was exactly as I remembered it.

She greeted me, and her voice was the same, too. I smiled and spoke back. We walked to each other, and we hugged each other hard.

And it seemed like it all washed away from both of us in that moment. The horror and the hurt and all the pain and darkness of long ago. I swore back when it happened that the pain of it would sear me inside forever. And in a sense, I guess it's always there somehow. It bubbles up now and then in the sadness of all the memories and all that was lost. But you can reach a place where you look back and realize you have grown beyond any point you ever thought you could have. And you can walk calmly through a new door as it opens, on a day you swore would never come.

It all seems so strange, but that's how it is. I can tell you that from where I've been.

We chatted for a minute, then walked into the house. In the kitchen, people were bustling about, getting the large feast ready. All of them smiled and welcomed me. Ellen and I sat at the table then. I kept glancing around. "Oh," she said. "Tim is upstairs, changing. He'll be down in a few minutes." And we just chatted along and caught up until I saw the man approaching from across the room. We are Facebook friends, so I recognized him. Tim. Ellen's husband.

I stood and held out my hand. He gripped it hard. We looked each other in the eye and smiled. "I'm happy to finally meet you," I said.

"Same here," he said. And he sat with us, and the three of us just talked about a lot of things. And when Ellen wandered away for a few minutes, Tim told me almost shyly that he'd read my book, and he liked to read my blog. I thanked him for taking the time. "I'm always honored," I said.

And soon the other guests began trickling in. I walked about, greeting the people I knew and introducing myself to those I didn't. When Ellen came around, I introduced her, too. "This is my ex-wife, Ellen." Some people looked startled, but mostly everyone seemed very OK with everything.

The evening came at us then. As we were getting seated, Ellen asked me, "Would you like to sit with us?" I hadn't really thought about it, but I accepted. "Yes, I'd like that very much." And we sat and ate together, the three of us. Me and Ellen and Tim.

Paul's White Party is a big, big deal. He and his people had prepared an enormous and delectable feast. Five or six courses, I can't remember. Salad, then soup. Then the main dishes, which included grilled salmon, lamb chops, and steak. The food was beyond delicious, the wine robustly red. And sitting right there, I sinned grievously with my feasting.

The hours wore on, and we were comfortable and relaxed. Right at eight, I told Ellen, "I need to leave now." And I told her the reasons why. She understood, and Tim did, too. I stood and he reached over, and we gripped hands again. I wished him well. And then Ellen asked, "Can I walk you to your truck?"

"You may," I said. I thanked Paul on the way out and waved good-bye to my other friends. I went inside to grab my keys, and Ellen met me in the garage. We walked over to the open door. And we stood there and looked at each other.

And we wished each other well. "I had a lovely time," I told her. "I enjoyed meeting Tim. He's a good man. I'm sure you guys have to work through things, like every couple does. But I wish you every blessing."

"Thank you," she said. "I had a lovely time, too."

We were done. There wasn't a whole lot more to say. We faced each other, and then we hugged.

"Good-bye," I said.

"Good-bye," she answered.

And then I turned and walked out to my truck.

WHISKEY AND ME

IT WAS A strange time in a lot of ways, the summer of 2017. A major stressor was draining a lot of energy from my life. The whiskey. It all hinged back to the whiskey. I had reached a place where a decision had to be made, where something different had to be done. Well. I was reaching that place, late that summer. I'm on the wrong road, here. I'm not young, anymore. Looking back, a few things are clear in retrospect. I was sick and tired of feeling sick and tired. I was overweight, bloated like a fatted hog. My face was swollen, my eyes were puffy. It was a hard and relentless slog, every day. Somehow, somewhere back there, I had chosen to embrace the one nemesis that can never be fully and finally slain. There had to be a better way.

It's always a choice. Everything you do is. And there is only one person in all creation who is responsible for your choices. You. Always. Talk to me about addiction all you want, and how tough that life is. It still boils down to how you choose to deal with the aftermath of your previous choices. And no, that's not harsh. It's just reality. I know what it is to be addicted. I know how hard it is. Trust me. I know, way better than I want to.

And I was hedging around, looking at the situation from every angle. Near as I could, anyway. Kind of poking at it, to see if any sleeping monsters would wake up. You calculate the cost, you make a choice. And this was a new door. That's what it was. A new door to a new road. And I could turn from it or walk through. It takes a while, to get to what you know is the right choice when you're standing in a place like that. At least, it does for me.

Sometimes you hear people say, when mentioning some-one who passed on, "He drank himself to death." And it is understood exactly what is meant by that statement. It's something like this: Oh. That kind of man. Yeah, he sure didn't have much self-control. He wasted his life away. He sure loved the bottle. He drank all that hard liquor. What a sinner. We can only hope he repented at the last second and maybe just squeaked through the door into heaven. Probably not, but we won't know for sure until we get there. If he made it, he's probably stuck in a little room way down in the basement somewhere. We'll have to go looking for him.

That's what people think to themselves and mutter to each other. Not me. I don't go there. I understand com-pletely when I hear that someone drank himself to death. I understand the pain and loss and bitter sorrow that such a person could not face. I know the monsters that lurk in the recesses of the mind and in the dark corners of the heart. I know, because I deal with my own demons of what was and what might have been. I've heard those voices calling in the night. I understand, because I poked my head through that door and looked around a bit. And I gotta say, it's not a terribly scary place. I wasn't frightened there, in that room where death is. I understand why people go there. And I understand why people choose to stay there.

It was just so hard to think about giving it all up. I had been close friends with the whiskey for a lot of years. More than twenty, I'd say. It's in my blood, it's in my genes, to crave that soothing amber fire. Much of my genetic attraction to alcohol comes from Mom's side of the family, that I've always known. We heard the stories about Uncle Joe Yoder and how hard he drank. And I remember when he died, at about my age. He drank himself to death. That was pretty much the accepted narrative. The Yoder blood was strong in a lot of ways, but it was flawed and weak in others. This I always knew, because it never was a closely guarded secret.

But it wasn't only the Yoders that the insatiable drive to drink came from. There was a strong pull from the Wagler side, too. Just not out in the open. The Yoders were honest about who they were. They had few pretensions. The Waglers, not so much. We never knew it, growing up, but there was a time when Dad nipped at the bottle, too. Way back in his younger days there in Daviess, he did. His older brother Ezra was always saddled with the burden and the shame of being the wild child, the renegade drinker in the family. Dad told me once that when Ezra came home from the Amish singing late on Sunday nights, he always threw his empty whiskey bottle onto a little ledge above the barn door when he took his horse in. (I can only imagine what kind of terrible rotgut it was that Ezra bought and drank. I'm sure it wasn't the single-malt scotch I got used to a generation later. I always thought it would be fun to knock back a few with the young Ezra of long ago. He could tell me lots of things I never knew.) There was a big pile of those empty bottles up there on that ledge, Dad told me. And I never thought to ask, What about you? Were some of those bottles yours? He'd tell you if you asked in the right spirit. He'd also sense it in a second if you were asking to try to nail him or trap him. And he wouldn't tell you, then.

We heard the furtive, whispered stories somewhere along the way. Long after we were adults and had left home, the first such whispers came. At least the first such whispers that I remember. And we poked and prodded and dug around a bit. Were the stories true? Looking back from where I am today, there is little question in my mind that there was a time when Dad was no stranger to the bottle. Way back in his younger years. The thing is, back in those days, I don't think it was all that big a deal if you drank a little. I think it was more of an accepted thing in the Amish Church, at least the Amish Church in Daviess County, for there to be whiskey in the house. So it wouldn't have been all that uncommon for a man like Dad to imbibe. He sure would have been predisposed to, if the whiskey sang to him like it sings to me.

Waglers and whiskey. It's a little startling to recognize that I'm not the first one of my blood to reach this door, to give it up. Because there is also no question that my father quit drinking, cold, long before I was ever born. He always talked against alcohol. Always wrote about how bad it was. Bad for your health and bad for your soul, too. That's what Dad believed. Maybe he was writing to himself as much as he was writing to his readers. I look at his life and his life's work, and I get some small grasp of the man's astonishing drive and strength. What he believed, he proclaimed boldly to his people, as no one had ever done before. He strode forward, confident and forceful and unafraid. What his hand found to do, he did with all his might. Such a man is who my father was.

That's where I come from, a place like that. None of it is any excuse for how far I went with the whiskey, of course. And I'm not making any. It's all about choices, whether you drink or don't. I don't judge it as a moral issue, even. It's simply a choice. As it was always a choice for me during those last twenty-odd years when I hit the bottle hard. A choice I never felt much inclined to change. Sure. There were a few dry spots in there, but those were aberrations. Mostly, I was content to hold it close, to embrace my good friend. To invite the brooding spirits in. I pretty much had to, I believed, after I started writing. I had to keep the bottle close, or the writing wouldn't come. Way down, I sure used that as an excuse to drink. And it didn't take much to fool myself into believing it was actually true.

And so it went. Until that summer of 2017. I talked to a few close friends about it. That was the first step looking back. Opening up to one or two friends I trusted enough to confide in. But I still don't know where the drive came from to go there in my head, to consider seriously what it might take to walk away. Maybe I was getting old and tired. Or maybe the Lord was nudging me along. He moves in mysterious ways, like the hymn says, His wonders to perform. I don't know why the resolve came to approach that door, let alone walk right up and step through. I just know it did.

It's always hard, when you're addicted to anything, to even think about giving it up. Doesn't matter what it is. Food. Cigarettes. Whiskey. Work. (Oh, and drugs, of course. Still. Real addictions are about so much more than just drugs.) It's scary and unnerving to force your mind to consider an alternative universe that doesn't include the thing you treasure so deeply in your heart. That idol you can't quite let go of. And this wasn't the first time I quit a habit that seemed impossible to break. I remember a similar place years and years ago. Back in my Amish days. Only it was cigarettes I was trying to shake off, back then. Not whiskey.

I remember the monsters of fear that snarled from the darkness. Don't even try. You're not strong enough. It wasn't the thought of not smoking for a day or a week or even a month. That wasn't what seemed so hopeless and overwhelming. It was the thought of not ever smoking again. Of giving it up forever. That was what was so brutally hard to look at in the face. The thought of never again waking up and sipping that first hot cup of strong black coffee and lighting a moist cigarette, dragging great draughts of delicious smoke deep into my lungs. Don Williams immortalized the ritual in his signature song, "Some Broken Hearts Never Mend": "Coffee, black. Cigarette. Start this day like all the rest."

I was in a strange place in my head that summer. A

strange road. Unfamiliar. I don't remember being scared much. Quietly desperate, I'd say, would be more like it. Large and fearful shadows loomed on every side, and they were closing in. A jungle. That's what it was like walking through. Or maybe wilderness would be a better word. It was a desolate place and dark, in my head.

It seemed like I was out there, stumbling through unfamiliar terrain. There was a new door, up there ahead. Beckoning. Calling. Beckoning. I knew a choice had to be made soon. And I knew the right one would be hard. Still. I was drawn to the new door by some magnetic force. Come. Step through. Make this choice. Do it. There had to be a resting place—there had to be. I could shield my eyes with my hand and see. Way out there on that other mountain, there it was. That place of peace I was looking for. I could see it. Out there, over the valley. Which could mean only one thing. That valley had to be walked through. I could see it and sense it. But still. What you know has to be done is the hardest thing to do. Often, that's how it is. And there I stood in the wilderness, in the jungle. Alone. Well, I sure felt alone.

And one day at work, I got to talking with some customers who stopped to pick up a few things. I'd known this particular couple for years. We chatted about this and that. And then one of them looked at me sharply. "How are you doing?" she asked. I guess she wouldn't have had to ask. She could tell. I was swollen and heavy, my face was bloated, and my eyes were puffy. Maybe she was just being polite. Or maybe she genuinely wanted to know. I figure she did. "I'm not doing all that great," I told them. And I didn't shrink from why. "The whiskey. It's getting to me. I love my scotch. And my vodka. Not an evening goes by that I don't drink. And yeah, I'm still taking my Superfood vitamins. That's probably one reason I'm still standing. But I'm kind of lost here. I have to do something about the whiskey. I'm not sure what or how. I've tried quitting before. Nothing has ever worked. You asked, so I'm telling you. That's how I am right now."

They stood there and looked at me, and something lit up in their eyes. And then they told me their stories. Way back when, they had both been exactly where I was. Hard-drinking bar hounds. And they had both quit, cold, decades and decades ago. Independently, before they even knew each other. Neither of them had touched a drop of alcohol since they'd sworn it off. And standing there talking to me that morning, they didn't spout wise, trite things like people do when they're preaching at you. They just told me what they had seen and lived. What had happened and how. I listened and I heard. Even at that moment, I sensed it was pretty amazing that two people such as this would show up in my life and tell me what they were telling me. These people had actually done what I knew I needed to do. Still. It sounded scary and a little hopeless. It would be a hard road. I listened as they talked. And I pondered their words in my heart.

It wasn't magic, the things my friends told me that day about how they had quit drinking. It didn't go like it always does in those nice stories that end with a sweet little moral lesson. I didn't swear off the demon rum by my mother's grave, and I didn't go home that night and never touch another drop. I simply absorbed the stories and thought over what my friends had said. Processed. Calculated. They had done a hard thing and made it stick. I wondered if I could do that hard thing, too.

That little incident made such an impression that I couldn't shake it from my mind. In the next week or so, I mentioned it to a few close friends. And it all fell into place, kind of on its own. I remember when it was one year since I had touched a drop of whiskey. I was astounded at how fast the time had whooshed by. And right then, I was focused on that milestone. One year. It was a big deal. The first full year on this broken new road. I had seen strange and beautiful things in that time. One year. And then I headed on out for the next one. *Today is all I got*, I thought to myself. *It's all I've ever had, and it's all I'm ever gonna have.*

And looking back over the long and lonely slabs of years that made up my journey to where I am today, I stand amazed at how many times it happened. How many times I despaired because of the hard road that stretched before me as far as the eye could see. How many times I felt lost, how many times I strayed far afield and could not find the way. And then, when it seemed like there was no door to open, here came a stranger or a friend, stepping from the shifting shadows. Here. This is the way. The right road. Walk this path. It has happened over and over. I don't know why I even get surprised anymore. But I do, because my faith is weak. Still. *Lord, I believe. Help my unbelief.*

And life goes on, as life does. Once in a while, as the day ends and night flows in, there comes a time when you feel pensive and your mind wanders to places it doesn't often go because it's just too hard. But you go there anyway, and you see the blurred face of someone you cared for more than anything, and you wonder why life went the way it did. And you feel it again like you mostly don't these days because you won't let your heart go down that path, not often, because, well, just because. Still, you sit there and absorb it one more time, the bitter sorrow of a loss so deep, you can't express it, you can't write it, you can't possibly speak it like it was. And you feel it all the way down, how alone you are.

Once in a while comes such a night as that. Now that I have a clear head.

There were times when I was about as unsupervised and unaccountable as I could have been. You always hear wise, trite things about accountability. How you got to have it to walk right with God. Well, I didn't have it. I'm not saying accountability is wrong. I'm all for it. But I am saying there are times when most of us slog along without it.

I remember how it was right after my marriage blew up. My world was bleak and desolate. And when you're stuck in such a world, you simply absorb the desolation around you. You feel it, taste it, hold it close to you. Trace it all the way down to its roots and then slowly start pushing it back. Working your way out. And that was me in those days. When I didn't feel like going to church, I didn't go. As Thomas Wolfe would say, Was all this lost? Or to rephrase Wolfe, Was all that a sin? To stay away from church when I otherwise could have gone? If you are sitting under preaching or teaching that such a thing is a sin, you are in bondage. I don't know of any clearer way to speak it.

I go to church regularly. Chestnut Church, out on Vintage Road in the country. There, I "assemble with believers" because I want to, not because it would be a sin if I didn't. And there at Chestnut Church, Pastor Mark Potter faithfully proclaims the gospel every Sunday. Patiently, persistently, joyfully, he proclaims. He keeps insisting that the church is a hospital, not a country club. And there is one particular refrain the man has hammered hard over the years, like a blacksmith at his forge. About addictions. Pastor Mark preaches like he always has. And he says, "When you are a child of God, nothing can ever make you not be. Nothing. And so it's safe to bring your problems to God. Tell Him. He's your father. He'll never get tired of listening. And if there are things in life too hard to face, if the pain is too intense, if you drown reality in alcohol or drugs, well, bring that to Him, too. Try to stop. Tell Him you want to. And try. If you fail, try again. Talk to Him again. And try again. And again. And again, and again."

In the summer of 2017, I was drinking as heavy as I had in a long time. Hard. Every day. And there were a few Sundays when I woke up and the last thing I wanted to do was go face anyone at church. I didn't feel guilty or anything. I just didn't feel good. Well, as you don't, when you're all bloated and sluggish. And so I just stayed home those Sundays. Slept in a bit, even though my sleep was extremely broken in those days. And by late afternoon, I was ready to head out and start the process all over again, to dull some of that intense inner pain. And I did, like clockwork. Every day.

And I often thought about it back then, hearing the good

pastor's words about talking to God and trying again and again. Yeah. A fat lot of good that's done me. Talking. Or trying. Over the years, I have tried and tried and tried to quit drinking. I even stopped cold a few times. The longest I ever quit was just over two years, back in 2006–2007. It was one of the last-ditch things I did to save my marriage. Quit drinking. It saved nothing. And after my world blew up, the lure of the whiskey, those shades of delicious amber fire, drew me right back to the bottle.

It's all so easy to rationalize, the reasons why. I have seen hard and broken roads and so much sorrow and loss. Plus, I write. Writers drink to dull the pain of what they have seen and lived. And relived, in the writing. The real ones do, anyway, the ones I like to read. (Or they did, back when they were alive. Thomas Wolfe drank heavily, right up to his extremely unfortunate and untimely end.) That's the crutch I used. And I settled in my cups, pouring vodka and scotch on the rocks from bottle after bottle, day after day, year after year.

What is right and what is wrong in a time like that? I don't know. I do know that Pastor Mark never told me I was sinning. He told me I was God's child and that nothing could make me not be. And he told me to try again. Not directly, not by getting in my face. But in his sermons, he told me. Try again. And again after that. And again. And again. It got so that I barely heard him when he spoke those repetitious words. Yes. It was nice that he thought God could or would help. But it just was what it was with the whiskey and me. We were connected for life, I figured. And sure, it was a choice. I never claimed or thought anything else. But it was a choice I didn't feel much motivated to change.

People around me could tell there was something going on inside me and that it wasn't going all that great. Nobody said much. Not until two close friends told me, separately and privately, "You are not well. Your eyes look bad. The whiskey's getting to you." The weird thing was, those two friends didn't even know each other. They still don't. That jolts you, to hear two voices saying the same thing from two completely different places like that. And you hesitate in midstride. You have to at least hear what was spoken to you. Is it true? Be honest with yourself. And right there it is, one of life's hard and fast rules. Be honest with yourself. I fought hard not to be.

Somehow, a few slivers of light penetrated my brain. Just enough so I drew back from that destructive door I was hell-bent on walking through. Stop. Make sure this is where you want to go before you step through. I mulled the thing over in my head for weeks. And I saw it. There. That other door is the one you want, not this one. And I wasn't real sure how to get from the wrong door to the right one. Or that I actually had what it took to open the right door once I got there.

I didn't set out on a big, majestic quest or anything. I just turned from the wrong door and stumbled along aimlessly, without a lot of hope in my heart. And then, one day, the right door inched open. And from somewhere, there came a mustard seed of faith. It was almost lackadaisical, how I chose to step through that door. I just decided one night. I was going to quit drinking until I got a better handle on things. That was it. There were no promises. No vows. Not to God. Not to myself. Not to anyone else. Just a simple, almost offhand decision.

And in the distance, the dragon of fear stood to block my passing, belching all the fire and smoke and noise and rage that only such a dragon can. I clutched my sword and tried to look brave. It was hard not to turn and flee.

The first few days were the fires of hell. Being dry, I mean. And the first few weeks, as well, in waves. The thought was constant, gnawing in my head. A drink. I need a drink. After work, it was all I could do to wrestle my truck straight home, instead of heading to the bar. Somehow, I hung in there. Almost immediately, the weight started washing from me. More than a pound a day. And that's what kept me on the right path early on, I think. The weight. I was ashamed and beyond weary of being a big fat slob. I was done being embarrassed at how I looked in polite company. *Never again.* That's what I told myself. That's what I thought. *I never want to be this slovenly again.*

Forty-five days. That's what my counselor told me years ago, when I was thinking about putting the bottle down for a season. Forty-five days is how long it takes for your body to break free from the physical effects of drinking. After that, you're clean. After that, you're free, if you can stay that way. So that's what I focused on there at the start. *Lord, let me have forty-five days of freedom. Let me get to that place. And then let come what may.*

The days moved on, then the weeks. And after six weeks or so, the pounds slid off a lot harder. I looked at the situation. And I thought to myself, *If you're gonna get down to the weight you want, you're going to have to starve yourself. I don't see any other way. And we all know what happens when you quit starving yourself. All that weight will come roaring back, the same as if you had never lost it. That's what happens.*

And so I was open to another road. And just about then, a good friend nudged me online. "Here," she said. "I've been walking this path over here, and it works pretty well. You should try it. I think it's exactly what you need." The path she pointed to? Intermittent fasting.

It was almost as lackadaisical as my decision to quit drinking was. I checked out the links she sent. Researched things a bit. Fasting is very much the "in" thing these days. It's trendy. But does it work? That was my only concern. And then I decided to do it. I went to eating one meal a day. It was no big deal. I'd never been a big eater. The alcohol was what had made me all bloated and heavy. So it was very simple for me to cut back to one meal a day. And the thing about that one meal is, there are no limits. For that meal, you can eat whatever you're hungry for, and as much of that as you want. Which is exactly what I've been doing for a long time now. Eating as much as I want of whatever I'm hungry for, once a day. I always finish off with a big old bowl of ice cream topped with butterscotch. That's the kind of "diet" I can wholeheartedly endorse.

I love it. The weight I lost before has stayed off, mostly. Plus a little bit more. Not that I weigh myself much. I've been shrinking where I need to shrink. My face is thinner than it's been in decades. I'm wearing jeans that had been stacked in the corner, never to fit me again. But they are fitting. My winter coats are getting baggy. I figure to make this a long-term lifestyle. Although, like the alcohol, the less I think about it or plan, the better it will go, I figure, too. I feel great. Actually, I feel fantastic. Better than I've felt in decades. And I feel it, breathe it, when I wake up every day.

Each morning is a new high.

BACK TO THE PRESENT

THE DAY AFTER Christmas, 2018. Up north and north we drove, me and my Jeep. Going to where Dad was. The phone rang soon after I hit the road. My older sister Rachel.

"Are you on the road?" she asked.

"Yep, I am. Heading on up." And she thanked me for going up there like I was. "It's OK," I said. "I want to go. Maybe he'll leave before I get there. If he does, I'm fine with that."

And halfway up Route 15, the phone rang again. My brother Titus. I answered and we spoke. He thanked me, too, for going to where Dad was. "I'm going to talk to him," I said to Titus. "I'm telling him it's OK to go."

Titus agreed. "I think you are the man to go see him," he said. "I'm glad you're going. Tell him I can't come. You are representing me, too."

"That's a great idea," I said. "I'll just tell him I'm here for all the boys. They can't come right now, so I'm here for them all."

202

We chatted a bit more, and Titus wished me well. "Keep us updated," he said.

I promised I would. Amish Black rolled on north into New York, then west toward Buffalo and the Peace Bridge.

I thought about a few other random things, too. I remembered what my Amish friend Levi had told me not long ago. His elderly mother had passed a few months before. He told me how the stress of caring for her had rolled off like a vast burden breaking free. "You don't realize," Levi had said to me. "You don't realize how stressed you are until someone like that passes on, and you no longer need to care for them. Physically care, I mean. Emotionally, you always care—don't matter the circumstances."

And I thought about what Levi had said, and I thought about how much care Dad had required over the past number of years. And Mom, too, before she died in 2014. She had to be cared for like a baby. Fed like one, too. And the vast bulk of that burden, whether it was fair or not, fell on one family. My oldest sister Rosemary and her husband, Joe Gascho. It was their family and their clan who took care of Mom and Dad in their final years. After Mom passed, they moved Dad's little house over to the farm of Rosemary's oldest son, Simon, on the southwest corner of the old community. And that's where Dad stayed when he was in Aylmer. Which was the majority of the time.

He took a tremendous, tremendous amount of care. And he was more than half-cranky much of the time. Old people get that way. I've wondered often, watching both my parents live into their nineties, Will there ever come a time when the Amish take their old people to live in an assisted-living facility somewhere? I think they should. Not knocking any part of the care Dad got, not at all. But still. The stress had to be intense. It just had to be. I guess I forget a little bit how nonnegotiable that whole issue is for the Amish. You take care of your own for as long as they are here. Period.

The border came at me right on schedule. And it wasn't all that backed up. I pulled up to the guard shack and handed over my US passport and my Canadian birth certificate. Like I always do on the way up. You can't keep me out, I'm telling them. I was born up here. (On the way back, of course, the Canadian birth certificate stays out of sight when I hand over my passport.) The guard was polite enough. Where was I going and how long did I expect to be in the country? "Not sure," I told him. "I'll be up for a few days, at least. Maybe a few days longer than that, if my father dies. He's in a coma. So I don't know." The guard handed back my papers and waved me through. And this time, if I remember correctly, the day was cloudy and cold when I drove into the land of my birth. Not sunny and clear, like it often was going up there.

I always take Highway 3 West. It's two-lane, but it's the most direct. It's six of one and half a dozen of the other, the time it takes to travel either route over to Aylmer. I take the two-lane road because I like it. And I moved along, making good time. At this rate, I'd be out at the farm where Dad lived a few minutes before four. And now my mind was not on little things. Now I was focused, getting close. Focused on getting emotionally steeled up for what I was about to walk into. It was a new place I'd never seen before, the place I was going to. And it was a new road, too, getting there. Amish Black pulsed along, holding steady in the light flow of traffic. Tillsonburg, coming up. That's getting close. Next town after that was Aylmer. Just east of Tillsonburg, there's a silly little traffic roundabout. I detest those things. I also know I'm getting real close to my original home turf when I pass through this one. It came and went. Onward, westward.

Carter Road was coming up. The next one would be Walker. That was where I'd turn, and then a mile or so to the drive that led to where Dad was. I signaled, then turned. The side road was paved, kind of. And driving along there, I did what I sometimes do when things are getting heavy in the air. I crossed myself. I admire and respect the sign of the cross as a gesture of communication with God. The Catholics got that one right. And I spoke in my heart to the Lord: *God, I don't know what exactly is coming at me. But you do. I know you are with me. Guide me. Guide my heart and guide my words. I trust you. I am not afraid.*

It was a long lane from the road back to the farm where Dad lived. And that lane was winding and bumpy and wet and muddy. I bounced along. As I neared the buildings, a long-top buggy came at me from the other way. The buggy pulled off into the grass as we got close. I stopped and rolled down my window. Who were these people?

The buggy door rolled open. It was my cousin Edwin Wagler, the elderly widower. He was one of Abner's older boys. The back door of the buggy opened, and Fannie Mae stepped out. She was Edwin's sister and my cousin, too, of course. Fannie Mae had been Dad's most faithful assistant with his writings and all four volumes of his latest works. She'd helped him get it together and keep it together, and she'd helped him get the books published and distributed all over the Amish world. It really was an astounding accomplishment for Dad, and he never would have gotten it done without Fannie Mae. I chatted very briefly with them both. Said hi, basically. And that I was here to see Dad. They assured me that my arrival was greatly anticipated at the house. I rolled up the window and drove on.

I'm trying to remember now. It was a few minutes before four when I pulled up to the buildings and parked my Jeep off to the side on the grass. And it was also basically dark. I hadn't connected that before, how dark it was that early. I walked across the yard and up the deck to the front door of my father's house. The place was well lit. I could see people in there. I opened the door and walked in. I was immediately greeted with a big hug from my sister Naomi. She had arrived a few days before, and she and Rosemary were here now with Dad. Rosemary came, too, hugged me. Both of them couldn't get done exclaiming, "We are so glad you came."

"Yes, yes," I said. "I wanted to, and here I am." I walked around and shook hands with a few others seated in the small room. My niece Ida Mae. Her sister Naomi with her husband, Peter. And then I was at the door of the tiny bedroom. The doorway, rather. There was no door. This was the room where Dad had always had his desk set up before. They'd made it into a bedroom. The old bedroom, where he had always slept before, the same exact room where Mom had died, that bedroom had a nice bed for the people who came to be with Dad to sleep on. Usually two people came, maybe husband and wife. And one of them slept while the other one sat up with Dad. Anyway, that was why the little house was laid out like it was when I got there.

I walked to the door to Dad's bedroom. Rosemary followed close behind. A small bed was there against the wall. Rosemary's husband, Joe, sat at the foot of the bed, on a chair. And I stood there at the head of the bed and looked down on the frail and wasted shell of the man who was my father. I didn't recoil. Well, inside I did. But outside, I tried hard to make it so no one would notice. He was on his back, covered with a thin blanket. You could see only his face. This was the way of all flesh. I barely recognized him. His beard was a mere wisp, curled under his chin. His cheeks were gaunt and sunken, his eyes were closed tight, and he gasped for air through his nose and mouth. Well, maybe *gasping* isn't the right word. He was breathing hard, as hard as I'd ever heard any man breathe. But he was breathing steady.

And the others in the house told him, with forced cheer, "Dad, Dad, Ira is here. Ira is here." They had told him I was coming. And they were pretty sure he had heard them. And now I was here. I went to the other side of the bed, tight against the wall. He could feel that hand, they said. So I held that hand in my own. It was scarred and old, his fingers frozen in place. But I squeezed it. "Dad, it's me. Ira. I came to see you." There was nothing, not a hint of response. I held his hand for a few moments, looking down on his tortured face, then gently set it on the bed. Somewhere about here, Simon and his wife, Kathleen, came over from the big house. They smiled and welcomed me. We shook hands.

And they told me, all of them, as we stood there looking down, how the man had suffered. He was on his back, they couldn't move him. There were sores. He had not eaten food in a week. And he'd had no water for the last three days. They could only swab his lips. If he swallowed water, it would instantly flood his lungs and drown him. This, then, was the ugliness of death. That was what Pastor Mark had called it, back when he prayed for Dad in church the Sunday morning before: "The family awaits the ugliness of death." This was it. This was what the pastor was talking about. I sat down on a chair at the head of the bed, almost in a daze. And just about right then, they started singing, the others in the house.

Their voices echoed through the small house, haunting, surreal, and beautiful. There were half a dozen people, maybe ten. And they were singing for my father in his pain. It was enough to make you weep. I know I wiped away a few tears. *Lord, look at this poor, tired, broken shell of a man. Look how he suffers. Can't you just come and take him?* "How beautiful heaven must be," they sang. *I sure hope it is, to make this worth it. Oh my. Look at how hard he works to draw the air in and push it out.* "There is rest, by and by," they sang. *How about sooner, rather than later, Lord?* "Some sweet day when life is o'er, we shall meet above," they sang. *Yes. Yes, we will. But, Lord, look how hard he suffers.*

Sometime, early on, I had mentioned that I wanted a little time alone with my father. Of course. No one made any fuss. And soon Rosemary told the others, "Let's go over to the house and give Ira a few minutes alone with Dad." They all filed out and walked across the deck to the big house. I waited until everyone had left and the front door had shut. Now. Now I was alone with Dad just like I'd asked for. I stood and held his hand on that side. His right hand. The unresponsive one. I stood there, looking down at the wasted shell of a body that was right on the threshold, right on the precipice of death's door.

There were no tears. I did not weep. I simply held my father's hand and looked down on his face. His eyes stayed closed, his mouth was open, and his labored breathing came steady but hard. It was work, every bit of air he drew into his lungs. I did not have a speech prepared. I knew what I wanted to say. The words would have to come on their own. And I simply spoke my heart in my native tongue. In our native tongue, the language I'd heard my mother speak from the moment of my birth. "Dad. It's me. Ira. I came to see you."

And I told him then, "I'm here for your sons. Titus told me to tell you he can't make it today. I'm here for him. I'm here for all the boys. They would come if they could. But they can't. It's time to go to where Mom is. You must go. There is nothing for you here, Dad, not anymore. You're suffering a lot. You must go to Mom. You have to go." And he may have been afraid. I don't know. He never made any motion, never indicated that he was afraid or that he heard a word I said. Still. I spoke calmingly. "*Du musht nett angst hava.* [You don't have to be afraid.] Mom is there, waiting. Jesus is there, too. You can go to them. Just let go. You have to let go, Dad. Let go of the pain. Let go and rest."

The others came back in soon. And I can't recall the exact sequence of things. In such an eventful moment, some details will be a little foggy. The small details, I mean. At some point, Simon's wife, Kathleen, came over with a great tray of food. And at some point, my sister Naomi's husband, Alvin, arrived from their home in Arkansas. Just pulled right in, in his big red Dodge pickup. Made me a little lonesome for Big Blue, that did. The pickup I'd had before my Jeep. Alvin was shown to Dad's room, just like I had been. He absorbed the brutal scene.

And then we all sat around and ate and talked and caught up. Soon, plans were made for the evening and that night. Alvin and Naomi would go get her luggage from Rosemary's, then go get a room at the Comfort Inn in Saint Thomas. Then they would come back to the house. At ten o'clock, my niece Naomi and her husband, Peter, would come, and my sister Naomi and her husband would leave. Meanwhile, my sister Rosemary and her husband, Joe, would stay with Dad until Alvin and Naomi got back around eight. And I chose to stay there in the house with them. I had just arrived. *Might as well hang out here with Dad. He's the man I came to see.*

People scattered. And then it was just me and Rosemary and Joe in the house with Dad. Just the three of us. Joe sat on a chair at the foot of the bed. I sat in a chair by Dad's head. Joe and I visited sporadically about this and that. Rosemary sat in the tiny living room just outside the door, a few feet away, facing me. I talked to them both, first facing Joe, then facing Rosemary. And I sighed, a little dramatically. The way Dad was breathing, he'd be around a few days. Of that I had no doubt whatsoever. I sighed again. And I told Joe, "Well, whatever happens, I'm here until it's over. I'm not going anywhere until Dad leaves."

Joe looked at me. Out of the corner of my eye, I noticed something. Dad had stopped breathing. He breathed again, then stopped. Rosemary looked in, staring keenly. "What's happening in there?" she asked sharply.

"He's not breathing," I said. I got to my feet. Joe did, too. Rosemary came through the door. We stood in line beside the bed, looking down at Dad. Me at his head. Rosemary in the middle. Joe at his feet. We stared at his face intently. Clearly, something unusual was going on. He breathed, then stopped. For what seemed like a long time but was only seconds, probably. Breathed, then stopped.

Rosemary turned to her husband. "Joe, go get the others," she said. Joe turned and disappeared. An instant later, the door slammed and he clumped across the deck to the big house, where Simon and Kathleen and their children were seated at the table, eating supper. My niece Ida Mae was with them. Joe ran up to the screen door. He never bothered to open it. He simply pounded hard. When everyone looked out, he motioned to them. Come. And he turned and ran back to the house. Everyone clamored after. In the back of my mind, I heard them rushing into the small kitchen toward us.

They filed in, Simon and Kathleen and Ida Mae and some of the children. And Joe. We all stood, close around the bed. Dad had gasped a few times when Rosemary and I stood there alone together. "He is dying," she said softly to me.

"Are you sure?" I asked. "He's quit breathing before, you all told me."

"Not like this," my sister half whispered back. "This is different." I looked at Dad's face. There was no recognition of anything, but simply an emaciated body gasping its last. The ugliness of death in a broken world, that's what was coming down right before us. A few small catches of air when everyone stood there around him.

We all saw him breathe his last breath. I had never seen a person die before, not up close like that. And now I watched my father leave. There was no struggle. He simply stopped breathing. Then his face set, and his body relaxed.

It was over. My father was dead. David L. Wagler had left his earthly body.

THE PAST AND
DAD'S HISTORY

DECEMBER 10, 1921. It was early winter, a long time ago. The cold winds swept in from the northwest and swirled through the raggedy little clapboard farmhouse, there in the Daviess countryside. Farmhouses back then were not insulated. It was just bare walls against the elements. I don't know if there was snow on the ground back on December 10, 1921. There easily might have been. I asked Dad a few times over the years, "What was the day like when you were born?" He always was vague about any specific details. Which means he never asked about it much and didn't know. Either that or the adults in his childhood world never took the time to tell him, because it wasn't important. Still. One can wonder from here. And one does.

The world was a vastly different place that many years ago. Unimaginably different. The murderous Great War had just ended a few years before. And the Spanish flu was just winding down, too, about the time Dad made his appearance. It was a hard place he was born into. It's probably about as much a miracle as it isn't, that he even survived at all. But he did. He was a sturdy son, of tough and hardy stock.

He was born into a family that had its own dark mark of shame to bear, though. The Waglers of Daviess County, Indiana. I'm not sure if my father heard much about it when he was young. I know he never spoke about any of it to us. There had to be whisperings and knowing looks and gossip during his childhood. There just had to be. There was a dark blot on the family name. It had happened barely a generation before. Dad's grandfather, his father's father, Christian, was a deeply disturbed man. The pure Wagler blood coursed through him. I know a little bit about that blood. Near as we can piece it together this many years later, he recoiled, mentally and emotionally, from the harsh realities of life around him. Until he simply could not take it anymore. He shot himself in the chest in 1891, at age thirty-six.

It was morbid, how he did it. He tied the gun to some saplings, ran a string from the trigger back around the sapling to his hand, and pulled the trigger. A very sick man, he told his young sons to come and see when they heard the shot, as he might have killed a "birdie." Dad's father, Joseph K., was one of those young boys who came running. The trauma of the scene was probably never fully wiped clean from the mind of the young man who grew up to be my grandfather.

At least Christian didn't physically hurt anyone else. A suicide is always a shameful thing in Plain cultures. There is dark sin buried somewhere, some curse from way back. That's what people think to themselves and mutter to each

suicide is not shameful; it's sad!

other. It was exponentially more shameful back then than it is now. It took a generation or two to even begin to live down the stain of such a deep shame as that.

Dad came along quite a few years after that stain was unleashed. And his father, Joseph K., had managed to work his way up in status to an upstanding member of the community, there in Daviess. He was somber, not given to silliness and cheap jokes. And he was a deacon in the church, yet. So the Wagler blood was struggling to return to respectability back in 1921.

Christian's widow, Mary, remarried and moved out of Daviess with her new husband. How she ever attracted another man remains a mystery to me. He had to come from a hard place, too, I always figured. He was from Mount Ayr, Indiana, and they moved to Nappanee after they got married. And Dad told me a little story once when we were talking.

He went on a trip with his father, Joseph K., and his mother, Mrs. Joseph K.—Sarah, I think her name was. They traveled on the train. Dad was five years old. So this would have been around 1926. The Roaring Twenties. I'm not sure where they went, but they stopped in Nappanee on the way home to visit Joseph K.'s mom, Christian's widow. They lived right there on the outskirts of town, Dad told me. He and his parents arrived one day and stayed overnight. The next morning, Dad decided to take a little walk there in Nappanee.

He strolled about in the fresh morning dew, a little Amish boy of five. Blithely skipped along. Dressed in a long-sleeved shirt and little barn-door pants and galluses,

I'm sure. And then he wanted to return to his grandmother's house. He lost track of which one it was, there in the row. The houses all looked the same to him. That's what he told me. And so he just walked right on into the house he thought was the right one. It wasn't. It was the wrong house. The woman of the place squawked in surprise to see a grubby little boy in her home. Dad was all embarrassed. He quickly ran out and over one house to the right place. I had never heard this story before. I wondered what the world looked like to a five-year-old child that morning long ago in Nappanee, Indiana.

The house is gone now, on the farm where my father was born and lived as a child. I mean, the house that was there then. A new house was built sometime in the 1960s, I think it was. And the old barn still stands. And the well and water pump out front along the fence, buried and unused in the weeds. Those are there. And the public school Dad attended as a young child. Parson's Corner. It's still there, right close to the farm. Not sure what it's being used for these days. But it still stands.

And that period of my father's life is about as blank to me as any. His young childhood. There were stories, I'm sure, that he told when I was growing up. I just don't remember many of them. Maybe I wasn't listening all that close. Still, in later years, I asked about that world. And Dad told me a little bit about it.

He saw the Great Depression before he was ten years old. I find that fact just astonishing today. That my parents both saw and lived through a window of history such as that. They saw the dust of the dirt roads in summer, and they saw the ragged tramps with knapsacks walking those roads to nowhere. They saw the peddlers traveling door to door in rickety vans, selling what they had to offer. The market came to the poor country folks back in those days. A sparse market, compared to what we now take for granted, but a market nonetheless. Dad spoke of the dry-goods man selling bolts of cloth for dresses and denim for Amish barn-door pants. Three yards of this, five yards of that. The man kept a running tally in his head, and when it came time to settle up, he had the total price all ready. He never made a mistake in figuring, Dad claimed. He was a real math whiz.

It's all a little foggy, those years in his life. And when he was a young man, those years are foggy, too. It's kind of funny. Dad wrote a lot in his lifetime. But he never spoke much about his childhood and young-adult years. Back in 2011, one of his sons got a memoir published. That son was me. *Growing Up Amish*. I told my story. And soon after that, Dad announced to his family that he had some notes he'd been keeping. He was fixing to come out with his own memoirs now, too. I chuckled when I heard it. That was great news. I'd love to read Dad's memories from when he was young. If that was what it took to get him going, his son getting a memoir published, then that was just fine. Dad envisioned a five-volume set of small books. He actually came out with four of those five volumes. The first two volumes were a gold mine to me. Most of the stories in them, I had never heard before. I'm glad he got them told.

Moving on, then, into his teenage years. That's when

he met Mom. At least that was what he remembered. Her father, John Yoder, had some livestock for sale. Some heifers. Dad was sent over to check the heifers out. I don't remember if he rode a horse or drove a buggy that day. He arrived at the farm. The sun was shining. Whistling a merry little tune, he walked up to the house and knocked on the door to see if any of the menfolk were around. The door opened. And there stood the most beautiful young woman Dad had ever seen. Ida Mae, it turned out her name was. Mom. She smiled at him, shyly and sweetly. Dad was tall and handsome enough, I suppose. He reflected his mother's blood and bone. Waglers are generally short. He was tall, with dark, curly hair. That morning, standing in the midday sun in front of that lovely young woman, Dad stammered and stuttered a little but got the words out. He had come to check out the heifers that were for sale.

Mom smiled at him again. He felt light-headed. She was so beautiful. And she told him the menfolk were all gone this morning. She was home with her Mom and sisters. The heifers were out behind the barn, if he wanted to check them out. Dad thanked her. He turned and walked out to the barn. The lovely young woman disappeared into the house. He checked out the heifers and reported back to his father, who later bought them.

That would have been in the late 1930s, probably. And Dad somehow found reasons to keep lurking around Mom's homeplace. They connected and started dating. And things moved right along. They were married in February 1942. They were very young when they started their journey through life together. And there was no way they could have known where the tides of life would sweep them as the years and then the decades rolled on like a flood.

And now Dad had been alone for a few years. After Mom passed away in early 2014, Dad spoke it. He'd never expected to last this long. His father, Joseph K., had passed away from heatstroke back in 1940. He was fifty-nine years old. Dad was nineteen. He didn't figure to reach the old age he got to. The Waglers just weren't known for their longevity that way. Maybe Dad got it from his Mom's side, from her Lengacher blood. I don't know.

Today, I look at who my father was in his lifetime. And I feel a tremendous sense of respect and pride. And yes, I know. He was a flawed man, of course. As we all are. I've gone there many times in my writings in the past. He was a hard, driven man. He was prone to extremes of rage and passion and desire. The road he chose to walk was his own. And no, he didn't treat Mom the best on that road. He treated her pretty bad a lot. She endured a lot of senseless suffering. Until she was approaching the end of her own road. Then he cared for her with gentle tenderness, desperately, eagerly, like a child trying to make up for past wrongs. He was such a man. I look unflinchingly and acknowledge his failures. Yes. He sure could have done a lot better. But still. He was so much more than the sum of his flaws.

He was a man. A giant of a man, whose footsteps will remain imprinted in the earth long after his passing. He was all the maddening things a man can be. Stubborn. Focused. Bullheaded. Flawed. Unyielding. Cold. And kind. Distant, yet he cared deeply for his family. He wanted what was best for his children, his sons and daughters. He walked the path that he believed was the right one. He wanted his children to walk that path, too. And he sacrificed his own desires to do what he felt was best for his family. Most notably, he moved from Aylmer to Bloomfield, way back in my youth. He did that so his remaining sons would stay with the Amish Church. It didn't work, of course. But he was willing to uproot all that he cherished and take the risk. And he did it.

He was adventurous. I don't know where my father, born of good solid Daviess blood, got his wanderlust. There was never any chance that Daviess would hold him. And once he forsook the land of his fathers, it was ever easier to leave the land he had fled to. I know his time as a conscientious objector in service camps during World War II vastly broadened his world. Later, it was a comparatively simple thing to move to Piketon, Ohio, then to Aylmer, then to Bloomfield. It's OK. He wasn't a nomad, but he didn't hesitate to travel to a new setting, a new world. There was always a place out there where things might go better. That's what my father believed, from what I can tell from his decisions.

He was a pioneer. My father will go down in history as one of the most visionary Amish intellectuals of all time. And yeah, I know. Some would claim that the term *Amish intellectual* is an oxymoron. I'll stand with those who say it's not. As I mentioned, Dad was a writer, which is a little bit rare in the Amish culture. And writing was the true passion and purpose of his life. In defense of the Amish way of life, he cranked out voluminous amounts of words, starting all the way back in his youth. He wrote because he had to, I suppose. I understand that. Compared to him, I got a real late start. And I'll never match his volume. Never. It wasn't until he followed his passion and his dream to launch *Family Life* that his name became legend among his people. I look at that one single accomplishment as the major defining event in his long and productive life.

Such a thing had never been done before, at least not with any measurable success. Sure, there were wild-eyed Amish guys here and there over the years, guys who cranked out a little rag of some kind. They were never successful. *The Budget* would be an exception, but that was a newsletter that depended on its readers to provide the letters to print. *Family Life* was a monthly magazine. With an editor and columnists and stories and serious historical research and such. And Dad threw all he had, all his energy and drive and talent, into making the venture work. It succeeded beyond his wildest dreams. I have always admired him tremendously for pursuing his vision. That took guts, it took courage, and it took a bucketload of faith.

He walked alone a lot. I can't say this for sure, but I've often thought it. Dad was a lonely man. He didn't connect easily or deeply with a lot of people. Oh, sure, he did on a surface level. He was a superb salesman. He could laugh and bow and scrape for a sale right with the best of them. But at a heart level, I think it was hard for him to connect with people. He had very few truly close friends, at least that I remember. I could be off a bit on this particular observation, but I don't think so. He was alone a lot, because you have to be in your head to really write.

I know this because that's how it goes for me. Writing is a lonely world.

And I thought about things as Dad got old. He went striding into his nineties like it was nothing. In the end, I guess, my father was a man as he walked through life. Dad. A figure so vast in my world that it seems futile to try to express it. But still. You do what you can. You speak as you are able to. You just keep walking.

"And you, my father, there on the sad height," Dylan Thomas wrote. "Curse, bless, me now with your fierce tears, I pray." Those words have always spoken to me. I know that in his last years, Dad saw the sad height of a lonely world. A world where others took him by the hand to lead him to a place where he may or may not have wanted to go. A world of loss and pain, where all but one or two of his peers were gone. I know he remembered life from long ago and looked back fondly on the days of his youth. I know he missed Mom. I know the road was long, and rough in places. And I know my father was weary and simply wanted to rest.

Tomorrow is promised no one. It will bring what it may. Today is today. We are here, and this is now. Today, we celebrate life and all that life is.

DAD'S FUNERAL AND
FINAL THOUGHTS

MY FATHER WAS dead. It takes a while to grasp such a thing when it happens. We stood there around the bed. Waves of relief swept through me. Dad was released. Right that second, Ida Mac, standing at the far end of the room, asked sharply, "What time is it?" She stepped out of the room to look at the clock. I pulled out my phone and turned it on. Precisely six thirty. That was when Dad passed on. I had been here for less than three hours.

I kept sagging with relief. Dad's suffering was finally over, after all this time. But I was suspicious, too. Paranoid, almost. I kept asking, "Do you think he'll start breathing again? You said before that he'd stop breathing for a long time, then start up." *Lord,* I thought. *Don't let him come back to this life of pain.* That's how intensely I wanted Dad to be released.

Rosemary reassured me. "No. It never was like this before." After five minutes or so, I stepped outside to make some calls. It was a good thing that my phone plan had been upgraded to international before I came over the border. I was sure gonna need this thing.

The first person I called was my sister Magdalena. She was the next in line in age after Rosemary. The phone rang and rang. Maddeningly, there was no answer. I tried Janice. She was probably with her mom. Again, no answer. I called my sister Rachel then. She was waiting. And I told her, "Dad passed away at six thirty."

"I'm so glad you were there," she said. And we talked. "You call Jesse and Rhoda. I'll call Stephen and leave a message for Titus and Joseph. You can post it on the family site," I said. She said she would, and we hung up. And we both made more calls to share the news. Our father had died. He no longer had any cares here on this earth. Finally, the time had come that he could leave.

I wasn't sure what the protocol was up there in Aylmer. The Canadian system. My nephew Simon dashed off somewhere to a phone to call the nurse and the undertaker. A few neighboring Amish people came and went. We sat around in the tiny house. Now and then I stepped outside to make a call or answer my phone. I had tried to call Alvin and Naomi, too. They couldn't be far away. The first time, there was no answer on Alvin's end. Ten minutes later, I called again. This time, there was a click, and he answered. And I didn't mess around. I told him, "This is Ira. Dad died."

There was a pause. "We're at the motel, getting a room," Alvin said. "We will be right out."

And that was the randomness of it all, and it just didn't seem right. Not that anyone could do anything about it.

Here my sister Naomi had come days before to help care for Dad. She had no wheels, the Amish trundled her around in a buggy. Those things aren't safe, in my opinion. She stayed out at Rosemary's house. Then she stepped away for a few minutes with her husband to go to Saint Thomas and get a room at the Comfort Inn. And right then, Dad died. Meanwhile, I had waltzed in for a little over two hours. And there I stood, closer to the man's head than anyone else when he passed away. I told Naomi, "I feel bad. I'm sorry you weren't here. There's nothing really that I can do about it." She was most gracious. No one can blame anyone for being where they were. It all just happened as it happened.

At some point, I left for Saint Thomas to book my room at the Comfort Inn. An hour or so later, I returned. Dad's body was still there. And around nine thirty or so, the lights of the hearse came bumping up the long lane. Joe Gascho stepped outside the house with a lamp to signal the hearse in. The big black vehicle backed up close to the front door, just off the deck. Two men dressed in long black coats got out and extracted a gurney from the hearse. They came clanking in and introduced themselves.

Joe showed them into the back room. They pulled the gurney in and set it beside the bed. Dad's body had stiffened some, you could tell. Joe stood at the doorway, holding the lamp high for light in the little bedroom. I peeked over his shoulder. The men lowered the gurney beside the bed, lifted Dad's body over, placed it in a large bag, and zipped it shut. Then they covered everything with a blanket. Rosemary handed them a bag as they clumped out through the kitchen. "Here are his clothes," she said. The clothes Dad would be buried in, all packed and ready to go. Joe stepped outside with his lamp. I followed him and watched as the gurney came out, pushed by one black-coated man and pulled by the other. They rolled it right up to the open door of the hearse, folded up the front wheels, and pushed it in. Then they shut the door. And out the long lane they drove into the darkness. I sure wouldn't want a job like that.

I remember, growing up, the words the Amish preachers often said at the beginning of a long service. Like Big Church or Ordnung's Church. Both went late into the afternoon. And I remember hearing the preacher hem and haw, getting started. Or the bishop, in Big Church. He would get up, clear his throat, and make a few noises about how humble he feels, standing up there, talking. Others could do it so much better. And then he would speak those fateful words. "We have a big field to cross today." Which basically meant that no one in that house was going anywhere soon. We were all trapped until the last second of the last minute of the last hour of the service. "We have a big field to cross." It's enough to send shivers down the spine of any Amish child. And that's what I feel like saying right here about the next few days leading up to and through to the other side of my father's funeral. We have a big field to cross. Maybe there are a few shortcuts. We'll see, I guess.

Thursday. First, there was a meeting with the undertakers at eight thirty. I'd never had much to do with funeral homes or undertakers. I drove Amish Black east on Route 3 to Aylmer, followed by Alvin and Naomi in Alvin's big red Dodge truck. I pulled in at the Tim Hortons there on the west edge of town. The drive-up window was deserted, oddly, so I pulled through and ordered a large coffee, black. It was thin and weak. I was disappointed in Tim Hortons. I thought you guys had decent brew. Naomi got out of the truck, and I cleaned off the passenger seat in my Jeep. We drove through town, to the east side of the main traffic light. And there, on the left, right at the end of the row of storefronts, it stood. H. A. Kebbel Funeral Home. It was kind of tight, getting in and out of the place. I pulled in, drove around the back, and parked on the east side, right up front outside the doors. "We won't be long," I told Naomi. We walked in. The large front room was empty. A bell must have rung in the back. The son of the father-son team stepped out and walked over to greet us. Bob, he'd told me the night before, when he was picking up Dad's body. He was very calm and smooth and efficient.

He led us to a back room, and we sat at a conference table. I handed him the envelope Rosemary had given me the night before. The obituary for our father. Rosemary and Naomi had written a rough draft in the past few days. I handed it to Bob, and we went over it. He took it to his office for his secretary to type up. And then we discussed the details of Dad's funeral. It would be on Sunday morning at nine a.m. I know it's a little horrifying to Lancaster County Amish, the thought of a funeral on a Sunday. But in most midwestern communities, it's not a big deal. For a funeral, Sunday works just as good as any other day. The funeral home would print up little folded paper obituaries to give to people who came to the viewing and the service.

Naomi and I checked out the potential covers for the notice. I liked the Dove of Peace. She liked a sunset scene. "Why don't we use both?" I asked. "Half of one, and half of the other." Bob the undertaker was most accommodating. He handed us draft copies of each. "We need to take this out to our sister's place," I told him. "We need approval. I'll be back later today to give you the go-ahead."

Bob's elderly father, Herb, came in to meet us, too. He was in his eighties, and he remembered when the Amish first settled in the Aylmer community in 1951. He remembered Dad from back then, he claimed. I know Dad's mom died in Aylmer. They took her body to Daviess by train. Herb was probably involved with all that. We chatted about his memories. And I pulled out a copy of my book then and signed it, to father and son. "This is about my experience growing up," I said. "Dad is a big character in the book, as you might imagine." They thanked me for my gift. An undertaker works with death every day, he sees it, lives it, and deals with it intimately. I wonder if they see and hear things that would freak out the rest of us. I wouldn't be surprised. But they are always so smooth and polished, at least the ones I've been around. Herb and Bob were no different.

Later that day, Naomi and I drove out to Joe and Rosemary's house. Everything is a bit of a jumble in my mind, as far as what happened exactly when. The details. We went over the little obituary notices, and I ran back to town with the final corrections. The funeral home people told me the copies would be ready to pick up at the printer's at four that afternoon. I rested at the motel and drove around a bit. Just before four, I stopped at the *Aylmer Express* offices. The printer's. They had two little boxes ready to go. I trundled on out to my sister's place. Somebody had dropped off food for supper, a large casserole. We would be eating around six, Rosemary said. After sipping black coffee all day, I was hungry for my meal. Around five, my brother Stephen and his wife, Wilma, came around. They had already checked in at the motel. The extended family was gathering. Most would arrive on Friday. I told Stephen, "Tomorrow morning at nine thirty, they are bringing Dad out to where the service will be. We might as well be waiting on him." Stephen agreed. We ate then. Later, I headed to my motel room. The first full day on-site was done. I slept fitfully that night.

Friday. This would be a big day. Well, all the days were big on that trip. You only got one father on this earth. It's a big deal to get together and bury him when he dies. I headed east into Aylmer and stopped for hot black coffee. McDonald's this time, and every time after that. A large for two bucks. Tim Hortons blew it with their thin weak water the day before. I headed east out of town, then north on Carter Road. Past the woods, then past the fields that had been the western edge of the farm I was born on. The western forty had been sold when we moved. A new homestead had been started by Omar Eicher and his wife back then. I'm not sure who lives at that place now. Might be English people. I drove on north to the next crossroad, where the school stood beside

the Herrfort farm. I crossed that intersection, and there
was the big gazebo-manufacturing warehouse where the
funeral would be. The exact same place where Mom's
funeral had been. It had stood empty and unused for a
few years. From what I heard, it took the menfolk a few
days to get it cleaned up nice.

I parked my Jeep out by the road and walked in. A
few people were busy getting ready. An Amish funeral is
an amazing event. A model of teamwork and efficiency. A
temporary kitchen had been set up in the office entrance
area. Cookstoves and tables, and a dozen married women
and single girls milled around. They would serve lunch
and supper today and for the next two days. Dad wasn't
here yet. The hearse should be out anytime. Stephen arrived, and Alvin and Naomi. I'm not sure if Rosemary was
there right then or not. I can't remember every detail of
every minute. I walked around, inspecting the place. Lots
of benches were already set up, with room for many more.
Some young men bustled busily about. They greeted me.
Asked my name. "I'm Ira," I said. They smiled, as if they
had heard that name before.

I stood around with the young men, and we talked.
Almost immediately, one of them got to telling me a
story. I didn't know his name. Later, I heard he was Paul
Stoll, son of the bishop Peter Stoll. And he told me. A
few years ago, Dad would drive around the community
in his own buggy. Back when he could still get around.
It was freedom, for him. Anyway, the young Stoll man
was driving along in his own buggy one summer day.
On the gravel road north of the graveyard. And off to

the side, there was a field of watermelons. Some local Amish farmer was raising them to sell. Dad had decided he could use a few of those watermelons, so he pulled in with his buggy and got out. It was no big deal. The owner certainly wasn't going to grumble if David Wagler stopped and picked a few melons.

And the young man told me he was watching when Dad stumbled and fell. Right out there in the field. He couldn't get up, so he started crawling along on his hands and knees toward his buggy. The young man stopped then, of course. He tied his horse to a post and walked out to help Dad get up. And there was my father, not particularly alarmed, moving toward his buggy as best he could. "There was David Wagler," the young man said. "Crawling toward his buggy on his hands and knees. And he was pushing three watermelons in front of him." I threw back my head and roared. If that's not a perfect picture of who Dad was, I don't know what is. I mean, he was going that way anyway. Might as well push along a few watermelons while he was at it. I told that story to my family many times over the next two days. We all howled every time.

Minutes later, the hearse arrived. Those things are always big and black and long and bulky and spooky. This one had taken a lot of bodies on a lot of last rides. Two attendants got out and opened the back door. I hadn't seen either one of them before. We greeted them and told them where to take the body. They pulled out a gurney. Dad was all covered up. They rolled him into the warehouse, then back into the little temporary plywood room where the coffin was set up. They disappeared behind the plywood. Stephen had arrived, and we lingered around. Waiting for the OK to walk in and see Dad. The attendants emerged ten minutes later or so and waved us in. Dad's face had looked sunken and wasted the last time I'd seen him. I was curious. Real curious. Could the undertakers work some magic?

Stephen and I walked into the little side room. The coffin was there, on two small sawhorses. We looked down at our father. He looked amazingly natural. His face had been filled out, however they do that, and his great beard was combed and fluffed and swept cleanly to his chest. He looked half-imposing, like he was going to get up and start managing things. Stephen and I stood there without a lot of words. Others drifted in, too, and stood around us. There were murmurs. "He looks good. So natural." And he did.

Friday was the viewing day for the locals. Anyone could come at any time, but the first day, it was just assumed that many people would be traveling to get there. So the locals come. Many came on both days. At noon, someone stood and announced that the food was ready. We all stood, and someone spoke a prayer, then people filed through. I didn't eat, of course. Just drank black coffee. I visited with many people that day. Two stood out to me. Joe Stoll and Bishop Ike Stoltzfus. I had a real nice long visit with Ike. But I sat with Joe first. He smiled and smiled. I'm sure a lot of memories were flooding through his head. He was my cousin and Dad's nephew, and he was in his eighties. He was also cofounder of Pathway Publishers with Dad.

And I asked him, "We always heard that it was out in the threshing field that you and Dad dreamed up your vision of Pathway. Is that true?"

Joe smiled again and settled in. "We were threshing at Johnny Gascho's farm," he said. Johnny is married to Joe's sister, Martha. "Your dad had the team and wagon, and I was out in the field with my pitchfork, loading. And every time your dad came out to the field with his wagon, I made sure that I was pitching for him." I listened, nodding. And he told me how they talked and schemed that day while threshing. Threw out their ideas. Later that next winter, he walked the half mile to my parents' house on a bitterly cold December evening. Jake Eicher came, too. The three of them had a meeting. The first one. Jake told Dad and Joe that he couldn't write, but he could keep the printing presses rolling. Jake offered an acre of land for the print shop. That night, my father's impossible dream was officially launched.

Joe told me one more little story. This one was from when he was a child of ten or so. Dad was at a Civilian Public Service (CPS) camp as a conscientious objector in World War II. Two of his married sisters, Mary and Anna, were living in Jerome, Michigan, at the time with their families. Anna, who was married to Peter Stoll, was Joe's mother. And Mary was married to Albert Stoll, who was Peter's older brother and Joe's uncle. The families got a letter from Dad when he was in the camp. The letter was typed. Typing was considered very modern back then. Somehow, Dad had taught himself how to operate the typewriter they had there at the camp. And Joe told me that Mary and Anna were deeply grieved that their younger brother was slipping so badly. So modern. They would have much preferred to just read his handwriting. I laughed and laughed. The Waglers were staunch Plain people, even way back then. They had hard blood. Dad never backed down, though, when his older sisters admonished him. He always, always typed his stuff. I can still hear the clack and ding of his old manual typewriter as he hammered away at all hours of the day and late into the night.

The day drifted on. The family arrived in spurts and fits. My sister Rachel, her husband Lester Yutzy, and many of their children flew into Detroit, then drove across the border from there. And soon after five, supper was served again. The thing about an Amish funeral is, everything is done for you. The food shows up, the funeral-service site is cleaned and organized and heated. The grave is dug by hand. The grieving family just sits back and experiences everything. It's beautiful. We ate then, and I was hungry. I loaded a plate with salad and hot food. Everything was delicious. One little side note, though: I don't think the Aylmer people eat a lot of meat, because it sure was sparse in those dishes. A tiny speck of ham floated around forlornly now and then. But it was all good. When you're getting fed like that, eat and appreciate. That's what I tried to do.

Magdalena and her husband, Ray Marner, arrived then. Jesse and Lynda had driven in from South Carolina earlier. And my family sat in two rows of chairs, facing each other, about eight feet apart or so. The line came down one side and back up the other and round and round. Sometimes it was busy, sometimes it wasn't. I chatted with Marvin and Rhoda, who had arrived from Kansas. Titus and Ruth arrived late in the afternoon with their boys. They had started off early that morning and made good time.

I repeated the story of Dad's death to all my siblings as they came. Teared up a bit, in the memory and the telling. And we hugged and spoke of who the man was and his vast, almost limitless impact on our lives. Our father. He was gone. It seemed surreal and impossible. He was survived by all his children. It was nip and tuck there more than a few times over the years. Almost, one or two of us went before him. But he never had to know a loss like that, even though he reached ninety-seven.

The youth came, too, after supper. Or maybe for supper. I can't remember. They came, dozens and dozens of single boys and girls. They sat in rows in the main part of the great room. And they sang. Aylmer never did allow singing in harmony or parts. The original bishop, Pete Yoder, claimed that God was more pleased if everyone sang in one voice. In one key. So that's what they do up there in Aylmer. And that night, it was beautiful. German songs first. Then English. And after half an hour or so, a minister stood with a German prayer book. I think it was Christian Stoll, Joe Stoll's youngest son. He spoke briefly, then asked everyone to stand. We did. He read a long German prayer aloud. I appreciated again the rituals and traditions of an Amish funeral. It's old, it's rare, and it's quiet and beautiful.

The youth all filed through to view Dad and to shake hands with us. And the crowd dispersed after a while. People left. Soon it was time for us to leave. And we gathered in the little plywood room with Dad, all the family.

His children who were there, and their children. We milled around a bit. "Why don't we sing a song?" someone asked. And Alvin Yutzy led a few verses. Some of the voices were cracked, like mine, but we sang: "I will meet you at the eastern gate, over there." We stood in somber silence then. Joe Gascho stepped up beside the head of the coffin, by the wall. It was time to close the hinged cover. (*Lid* seems a little harsh. So *hinged cover* it is.) And he said somberly, "It's time to close the coffin. Titus, will you help me?" And Titus rolled up, and he and Joe gently lifted the cover and set it down. Rituals and traditions. We filed out.

I drove to the motel soon. Almost everyone from out of town was booked there. The first night after Dad passed, I came in and chatted with the Indian owner. They had been told there was a funeral coming soon. Rooms would be needed. So they were looking for us. I got there that night and stood at the counter. Wagler funeral. What kind of discount can you give? Deal with me now. I got lots of family and friends coming in over the next few days. He gave me 10 percent off. I could barely get my room booked, because the phone kept interrupting us with my kin calling for reservations. We got it done eventually. The phone kept ringing. "I wasn't kidding," I told the man. My room was very nice. Recently remodeled. Clean as clean could be. The bed was firm, just as I like it. That first night, I hung out my clothes for an extended stay.

We gathered in the conference room then. All the Waglers and their kin and their friends. I had asked the owner, back the first day, "Can we use the conference room every night? And make sure to rent the rooms around the conference room to my people, so no one gets upset." He claimed he would. It didn't quite work like he'd promised, but in the end, everything went pretty well, considering. Loud times were had. Calls were made to the front desk with irate complaints. Warnings were issued and it got quieter for a while until it wasn't anymore. My people don't take all that kindly to being shushed. We tend to get louder.

Saturday. Moving along, about as slow as the actual days went. Every minute was loaded with so much. Emotions. Memories. Meeting old friends. It almost becomes a blur. Rosemary wanted us out at the viewing around eleven. I meandered out with my old friend and brother-in-law Marvin Yutzy. We always like to take a few minutes and talk alone. We chatted as we cruised around the community. I took him around the block from the east, past our old homeplace. Only two buildings remained from my childhood days there. The vast old frame barn and the block washhouse. Oh, and the old shop and machinery shed. We had just built that shed new the year we left. So only three actual physical things remained. It was like a different place. Still, I pointed out the pond where we'd played hockey and the north banks where I'd caught my first little mud catfish when I was about four. My sisters Rachel and Naomi had taken me fishing for the first time. I pointed out that spot.

This day was pretty much a repeat of the day before, except there were more people. Friday was a little slow. Saturday was much busier. Everyone arrived from my family, the ones who'd had to travel a distance. All of them got there by Saturday afternoon sometime. My brother Joseph came with his wife, Iva, accompanied by several of his sons and his youngest daughter, Rosanna. He was quite ill from multiple myeloma, which he had battled for ten years. Not doing that well. He could walk some, his family also pushed him around in a wheelchair. He didn't shake hands with anyone. He had to be extra careful about infections and germs. We welcomed every one of them as they came. This was it. This was Dad's funeral. We would all make it. A lot of the grandchildren, my nieces and nephews, showed up, too. There are fifty-nine. Not all could make it, of course. But a lot did. Alvin and Naomi's son Gideon Yutzy and his wife, Esther, and their infant youngest daughter flew over from their home in Ireland. From Dublin to Toronto. It used to be that people couldn't go more than a few hundred miles for a funeral, what with news traveling slow and transportation issues. Now you can fly in from anywhere in the world, if you're of a mind to.

I invited three people by personally reaching out to them. Jerry Eicher, my cousin and author friend. John Schmid, the folk singer from Holmes County, Ohio. And Mark Ernest Burr, whom I last saw when I was a child in Aylmer. He was one of those "wacky" English converts who had in mind to join the Amish. It didn't work. We'd reconnected online, Mark and my family, and it felt right to invite an old friend from another time to my father's funeral. I told Schmid about it because he'd gotten to know Dad down in Florida. In Pinecraft, at Birky Square, where the singers come around every winter to play their stuff. Dad had loved John's singing. He went to all his concerts that he could make. He particularly loved John's ballad about Howard Gray, a boy who was bullied like Nicholas was in my first book. Dad always requested that song when he saw John singing. It's pretty ironic, when you think about who my father was in my childhood, that he would openly listen to and enjoy any musical instruments. It was always in there, that desire and enjoyment. He just quashed it for many decades. It is what it is, I guess. Or was what it was.

I invited those three people, not that anyone else would not have been welcome. In most Amish communities, you don't need an invite to go to a funeral. Lancaster and its daughter settlements are the exceptions. Before I moved to Lancaster, I'd never heard of having to be invited to a funeral before you go. You just went if you wanted to. I was happy that all three of my friends showed up. Jerry and his wife came on Saturday. John and Mark didn't make it to the funeral site until Sunday morning. I chatted with Jerry after we ate supper Saturday night. Another delicious but meat-challenged casserole. Jerry was strolling around, and I waved him toward a seat beside me. I thanked him for coming. He said he'd been seriously considering it, then my text had made the final decision for him. And we just caught up. I always ask for his take on the publishing world. The man has been around and has seen a lot. I respect his opinions. He asked how my book was coming along, of course. "It's coming slow," I said. "The thing is, I've known for a while now that there will be no closure for the book until we bury my father. Now that's happening. Now I guess we'll see what comes. I don't know."

Jerry nodded. And he told me again, like he'd said

before, "You should get a book published of a bunch of your best blogs. That would sell."

I looked dubious. I listened, though.

And he spoke about my father, too, Jerry did. He told me, "Your dad was way more influential than people realize. He had a tremendous impact."

"Yes," I said. "I know that."

Jerry went on. "Your father was flawed, and he knew it. He knew he was writing about the ideal, not reality. He knew that. He did it deliberately." And Jerry made a fascinating observation. He has written a lot of Amish fiction in his time. More than a million copies of his books have sold. That's a lot. And he told me that when he did research on some Amish community somewhere to get materials for a new novel, he soon noticed something. If an Amish community allowed its people to subscribe to the Pathway publications, like *Family Life*, that community had higher moral standards than the communities that didn't allow the magazines. There was a clear distinction, Jerry claimed. The plainer hard-core communities always had more issues with bed courtship, alcoholism, and just overall corrupt morals. He mentioned tobacco, too. But I don't consider tobacco immoral, so I don't count it as a corrupt influence in any Amish community.

And Jerry told me, "That was your dad's work, right there, those communities with the higher morals. That's the vision they had at Pathway. That's what they were trying to do."

After the youth sang at the viewing, we stood around the coffin one last time as a family and sang a few verses of another song. Alvin Yutzy led us as we sang: "As I dream of a city I have not seen." And after that, we all headed to the motel. The crowd was bigger than the night before. There was food and feasting. And much noise again. I think they kept it down that night, so no one got kicked out of anywhere. I went to bed a little late. Set the alarm for early. Tomorrow was the day. Tomorrow we would return my father to the earth.

Sunday. The big day. I got up before six. Cleaned up and shaved and dressed in my black suit. The one I'd gotten married in. I couldn't get the thing on for years there, back when I was drinking hard. Way too much bloated weight. After eating one meal a day (OMAD) for a few months, I fit right into it again. Well, and after quitting drinking. I buttoned up a clean white shirt. No tie, though. I like to wear a tie to church at home, and to other places where it's fitting to do so. A lot of ex-Amish won't wear a tie to an Amish funeral. There's just something about it. The people at home, your people, they'll know you're just showing off if you wear one. Getting a little fancy there, eh? No one would say anything. But they'd think things. And this is one of those rare instances where you don't do something you otherwise would have, purely out of respect for your hosts. I am free to not wear a tie. That's how I see it. And that's how I dressed. Black suit, with folded-back English lapels, of course. White shirt, buttoned to the top. And no tie. I shrugged into my trench coat and walked out front to the lobby, where a good many of my family were flitting about, eating breakfast and making noises to go to a funeral.

My nephew Ivan Gascho had stopped over in London

that morning to pick up my brother Nathan. They were coming to the motel, and Nathan was driving out to the funeral with me. They arrived, and I hugged my brother. Welcome. He spiffed up a bit in my room. It was time to go. We walked outside into about three inches of fresh, fluffy snow. It had come down the night before. And now a chill wind blew. I huddled in my trench coat and buckled the strap across my waist. Nathan and I boarded Amish Black. It was cold, it was wet, and the roads were slick. Thank God, now, for my Jeep. We turned north off the highway to bypass Aylmer and kept pushing east. East, through the community. East, to the funeral.

We parked and got out and walked in. The winds whipped cold around us. Nathan had invited his old friend Juanita Staken to the funeral to sit with him. She had already arrived. We took our seats with the family. I looked around. The great warehouse was filled with people. Benches and benches and rows of people. The little plywood viewing room had been dismantled, that space was now covered with benches. Over by the eastern wall sat the preachers in a row. Dad's coffin was there in front of them, covered with a clean white cloth. People filed in and filed in. It seemed like everyone was seated. It was ten minutes before nine. All was silent, and the place was full. And then the first preacher stood to preach.

It was Simon Wagler, my cousin and Dad's nephew. The one who drove with Dad past the graveyard, when Dad said he could hear them calling him, the people buried there. The family had picked Simon to have one of the short first sermons. There would be three preachers, two would preach short and one would preach long. There are some politics involved in choosing who gets to preach at an Amish funeral. And that's about all I got to say about that. Anyway, the family had decided to ask Simon to preach, because he had been so kind to Dad over the years. And the day after Dad passed, I was dispatched to go track Simon down and ask him.

I'd pulled into his drive sometime around late morning. Someone there told me that Simon had gone over to one of his other farms to drop off some things. I knew where it was, so I headed over. Just a half mile down the road. A truck was parked outside close to the shop. And I heard someone banging around inside, moving things. I walked in. Simon looked over and recognized me. We shook hands. Visited a bit, then got right down to business. I told him then. "I was sent here to ask you a favor. Would you preach at Dad's funeral? It'll be the first sermon or the middle."

Simon acted very surprised and humble. "Well," he said. "There are certainly others who could do it better than I could. But if you ask me to, I will be willing to preach."

"Thanks," I said. "That's what I needed to know." We shook hands again, and I left to tell my family, "Simon agreed to preach. I asked him. He said he would."

And now he stood, facing the crowd in the large warehouse, hands clasped to his chest. He never was a magical speaker, not golden tongued, like some. But he spoke loud and clear. And he spoke of some of his memories of Uncle Dave. "Now our brother has passed on." He mentioned the graveyard incident, how Dad had heard the voices calling. Simon was taking Dad somewhere in the buggy, and they passed the Amish graveyard. Dad turned to Simon, tears running down his cheeks. "I can hear them calling me," he said. "I can hear the voices calling me." The clock was on the wall just above the preacher's head, where everyone could see it except the one who was standing and speaking. I felt a little bad for Simon as he stopped and turned his head and craned his neck to check the time. He spoke for around fifteen minutes. Then he shut down abruptly and took his seat.

Next up was my cousin Kenny Wagler from Daviess. I'd met Kenny and his father, Wally, before. Back a few summers ago. Full-blooded Daviess people, they are. Kenny preached in a loud clear voice for about fifteen minutes or so. He quoted a lot of Old High German hymns and other poems. He craned his neck, too, to look at the clock behind and above him. Every preacher should be able to clearly see some sort of clock. Oh well. These guys all made it through OK. Kenny took his seat then. And the third and final preacher stood and faced the assembled people.

Sam Schrock had come with a van load from Bloomfield, Iowa, the place we'd moved to when we'd left Aylmer many decades ago. Sam and his family had moved to Bloomfield long after I'd fled the place. From somewhere in Oklahoma, I think. Sam is a bishop there in Bloomfield, one of many. He knew Dad from when my parents still lived there a dozen years or more ago. They were friends. He had many memories of Dad. He spoke in a clear, cutting voice that reached every crevice of the vast warehouse. He preached for a solid hour. That's a long time for a funeral sermon. I figure the presiding bishop probably told Sam to just go ahead and take his time. Talk for an hour. The thing is, Dad would have approved. He liked long sermons, or claimed to. A trait that bypassed most of his children, I think. It was all good, I guess. There is no testimony after an Amish funeral sermon, except in some odd places like Kalona, Iowa, where the preachers ramble on incessantly. Not in Aylmer. After a final, rather lengthy prayer, Sam wrapped it up sometime around ten thirty. Then the casket was opened for the official viewing. And the people started filing through.

A preacher stood off to the side and read Scripture aloud in German. And then another preacher read some old German hymns. People filed through by the hundreds. It's always fascinating to me, how the Amish will bring their young children to a funeral. Death is a part of life. It will come for us all. This is stamped into a child's mind from earliest memory. And I saw it again here. A father or a mother lifting a young child so the child could see the body. My father, in this case. The little children stared and stared, then moved on with their parents. I'm sure some psychologist somewhere would say this is not healthy for young children, to see death up close like that. It's how the Amish have always done it. I respect that tradition a lot.

I never heard an official count. Offhand, I'd guess there were around eight hundred people there. Hundreds more had walked through in the two days of viewings. Old Bloomfield was well represented. The people who had lived in Bloomfield way back when we first moved in. I won't go naming names, because I'd miss someone.

Another time and place, maybe. The family had looked forward to welcoming Mrs. Rachel Graber, Dad's younger sister and only surviving sibling. She was ninety-four and lived in Kalona, Iowa. At the last moment, the widow Rachel had some sort of spell, and she couldn't make it. We were of course disappointed. She would have been given a seat of high honor. Had the funeral been in the states, where people didn't need to hassle with getting over the border and back, I'd guess there would have been a lot more attending. You can't know for sure. But I'd say there would have been. The lines filed through. And then it was time for the family to get up and see Dad one more time.

I hadn't paid any attention to how this would all come down. I know my sister Rachel badly wanted each of Dad's children, one at a time, from oldest to youngest, to view Dad with their spouse and children. That hadn't happened at Mom's funeral. Not sure why. Like I said, I just never concerned myself with any of those matters. I figured me and Nathan could always go up together, or something. Anyway, that's how they decided to do it. One complete family at a time. Rosemary got to her feet. Joe stood, too. They walked the few steps to the coffin and stood looking down at Dad. And their children and their families came up and surrounded the coffin with their parents. A few families at a time. Joe and Rosemary had a lot of offspring there that day. The most of any in the family. It took some minutes for everyone to circle through. Then Joe and Rosemary sat back down.

Magdalena and Ray Marner were next. And Janice, who

had flown in the night before. Magdalena had whispered to me when we got to our seats, "You and Nathan and Juanita can come up with us. We're only a few people. So now I stood. Nathan stood, too, then Juanita. Janice came walking from a little way across the aisle. And we all gathered around my father's coffin. We huddled in a group and held each other close. We looked down on that strong, stern visage, and we all remembered. A minute or two, and we turned and walked back to our seats. Joseph's family was next. His sons pushed him up in a wheelchair. Then Naomi and Alvin and all their children came. Then Jesse and Lynda and their sons, Ronald and Howard. Then Rachel and Lester and all their sons and daughters. Then Stephen and Wilma and all their children. Then Titus and Ruth with their sons, Robert and Thomas. And then Marvin and Rhoda at the end with their children. It took some time. There were tears, but they were mostly quiet tears. After the last of us was seated, the pallbearers stepped forward. Four of them. Youngish men, in their forties, I'd say. They stood at each corner of the coffin as it was closed. Then they lifted it by hand and carried it past us, out the door to the west.

We milled around then as the body was placed in a hearse buggy and the procession slowly drove out to the road and headed west. I got in my Jeep and drove south around the block. Then up the main drag west, then back north to the graveyard. I was among the first to get there. I parked Amish Black directly across the road. Just a bit back from even with the gate. And there I sat. It was bitterly, bitterly cold outside. I dug into a pile on the back seat and found a big thick stocking cap. I would take that with me, in case my head got too cold. Other vehicles flowed in then from both directions and parked all around on the side of the road. Huddled in my trench coat, I walked out to the grave and stood there with a few of my brothers and nephews. The hole had been covered overnight to keep the snow out. The men lifted the plywood and the planks and set them aside. We stood, looking down at the rough wooden box that would hold the coffin.

My brother Jesse and his sons had stopped the day before, when the men were digging the grave by hand with shovels. Jesse and his boys got down and helped dig for a bit. When I stopped a few hours later, the hole was pretty much done. The four Amish men showed me, there at the bottom. Dad's grave was very close to Mom's, a mere two feet away, if that. The earth had caved in down at the bottom. The men pointed it out to me. You could easily poke a stick in there and hit the rough box that held Mom's coffin. Not that anyone did. It never occurred to me that anyone would. Wasn't tempting at all. Still. That's how close my parents would rest together in the earth. David L. Wagler and his wife, Ida Mae (Yoder) Wagler.

And way up north, around the corner, came snaking a long, slow line of buggies. The lead buggy got there eventually and pulled off to the side a little, just outside the gate. The buggy stopped. Some men emerged. One held the horse. The pallbearers came and opened the rear door. They pulled out the coffin. Timothy Stoll, the funeral director, took the two sawhorses from the buggy and led the pallbearers into the yard. About halfway across, they stopped and set the coffin up. There would be one last quick viewing in the bitter December cold.

The coffin was opened, and people filed through one more time. The last time. They walked by on both sides, so it didn't take long. And here, I'll say this: pretty much everything that happened to me on this trip was unplanned. You can't control events. You just walk. I was sitting in my Jeep across the road, staying warm and watching things. Watching people file past and gather over on the left by the gaping hole in the ground. About then, my nephew Titus Aden Yutzy came strolling by. Rachel and Lester's second son. A talented auctioneer, he is in high demand in his home area. A good auctioneer is like a good preacher. It's easy to listen to either one. Titus had flown in late the night before, because there was a wedding back in Kansas in his wife's family. As soon as he could get away, he hopped a plane to Detroit and drove over. He was determined to see Grandpa Wagler one last time.

I rolled down my window as he walked up. We chatted. And he kind of grinned at me. "Are you going to put a pen in Grandpa's hand?" he asked. I just looked at him. It didn't register for a second, what he was saying. A pen? In Dad's hand? And it hit me. Yes. What a grand idea. A pen. The writer would be buried holding a pen. Dad's older sisters would be pleased that it wasn't a mini-typewriter, or something scandalous like that.

"You know what?" I said. "That's a great idea. I have a pen right here." I had carried it the last two days, along with a little notepad from the Belmont Inn in Abbeville, South Carolina. I had stayed there a few years ago when my nephew Steven Marner and his wife, Evonda, had their wedding reception there in town. It was an artsy little notebook with a plain little artsy pen attached to one side. I had actually taken some notes the last few days, a thing I rarely do. I just knew the event was too huge to try to recall from memory later. Now I had a pen for Dad. "I'm going to do it," I said to Titus Aden.

Minutes later, most of the crowd had passed through. A few still lingered. A few more minutes and the hinged cover would be closed forever. The screws would be driven down hard, hard and final. I walked through the gate into the yard. Janice met me there. I told her, "I'm putting this pen in Dad's hand. Where's Howard? Is he close?" Janice went to find my nephew and her cousin Howard Wagler. Jesse's youngest son. He came over with Janice, and the three of us walked across the trampled snow up to where my father lay. We stood around close. No one seemed to notice. I reached down and slipped the pen into Dad's hand. I thought about it as we were turning away. It's in his left hand. That's the wrong one.

The crowd ebbed and flowed past the coffin. I kept thinking about that pen I had stuck in Dad's left hand. And I watched for my chance, waiting until no one was close. Then I walked up alone and picked up the pen and placed it carefully in Dad's hand again. The right hand this time. It seemed like the right thing to do. Either one would have been OK, I learned later. Dad was born left-handed. He was forced to use his right hand, trained that way as a small child. That was probably a brutal thing for him. I didn't remember knowing that before.

Timothy Stoll stepped up to close the cover. I watched intently from nearby, just to make sure nobody snuck that pen out of there. A last glance at my father's face, and then the door was firmly shut on Dad's dark new house. The screws were turned by hand and driven in tight and hard. It was almost anticlimactic. I had seen and felt so many things so intensely that this moment seemed surreal. The family hovered around the open grave. Outside the fence, a large van had pulled up close and parked. Titus sat in the passenger seat and watched from the warmth.

The pallbearers approached. The four men who had carried Dad out from the service. They now picked him up with crossed boards and carried him over to the open grave. They set the coffin above the hole on those boards and placed their straps under. They lifted ever so gently, the boards were removed, and down, down into the earth went the wooden box that held my father. Back came the straps, and down went the lid of the rough box the coffin was placed in. I waited for two of the men to step down into the hole, on the box. They always hand down the first shovels of earth and gently place it all around. It didn't happen. First time I saw that at an Aylmer funeral. The men took shovels and threw in the dirt from the top. Gently at first, until the box was covered. Then they shoveled hard. And then the family stepped in to help.

It was random and relaxed. I took a turn, then Stephen and Jesse did, too. And a bunch of the nephews and nieces. Some of my sisters stepped up, too. And we got Dad settled into his dark new house, where the winds are always silent (paraphrasing Thomas Wolfe, there). After the grave was filled, Bishop Peter Stoll spoke briefly in a great booming voice. That man can sure preach. He spoke loudly and solidly and clearly for five minutes or more. The crowd drifted away then. We stood around and sang some songs, the family and a few others. The old hymns that Dad loved. We sang them to him for the last time.

After the last person had walked out of the graveyard, my brother Jesse stood by the gate. He swung it shut and wrapped the chain around the post and latched it back. A symbolic gesture from one of my father's sons, the oldest son who was physically able. The gate had closed. It was the end of an era.

We all returned to the big warehouse, where a noon meal was served. I sipped black coffee and mingled. And I couldn't help thinking about it. The Aylmer Amish community came through. They were weighed, the people there, and not found wanting. They sure know how to host a large funeral in that place. They also know how to offer hospitality. I thank every single person involved. All the cooks, the people behind the scenes, the pallbearers, and the preachers who preached. It was a big deal to get my father buried.

And here, I thank my sister Rosemary and her family one more time. Thank you for so tirelessly taking care of our father in his old, old age. Right into the sunset, right into the twilight. It was a long hard road, and a tiring one. All of you deserve some rest.

And now we reach the end. The warrior has laid down his sword. And now, at last, he sleeps. Right there beside Mom in the graveyard in the Aylmer community. The place his heart never left. The Amish world has lost a giant. His kind will not soon come again. We gathered from all around, his sons and daughters and much of the extended family. We gathered, we remembered, and we mourned. And we buried the patriarch of our clan.

David L. Wagler, your journey was a long one. Rest in peace, my father.

ACKNOWLEDGMENTS

Special thanks to:

Virginia Bhashkar, my editor. Thanks for seeing my vision and making it happen.

Ellen. We tried and tried. It didn't work. That's OK.

Chip MacGregor, my agent and friend. Thanks for another open door.

My extended Wagler clan. Thanks for your unfailing support and love.

Reuben. My old friend. The power of the gospel is a beautiful thing.

ABOUT THE AUTHOR

Ira Wagler is the *New York Times* bestselling author of *Growing Up Amish*, which has sold more than 185,000 copies. He is beloved for his vivid depictions of Amish life, as well as his ability to touch those who pursue their own heart's calling amid resistance. His popular blog has received more than one million unique visitors and gains thousands of new readers each year. Originally from Aylmer, Ontario, Ira now resides in Lancaster County, Pennsylvania. Read his blog at www.irawagler.com.